Dress Like a Parisian

Aloïs Guinut

Dress Like a Parisian

An Hachette UK Company
www.hachette.co.uk

First published in Great Britain in 2018 by Mitchell Beazley,
a division of Octopus Publishing Group Ltd
Carmelite House, 50 Victoria Embankment
London EC4Y 0DZ
www.octopusbooks.co.uk

Distributed in the US by Hachette Book Group
1290 Avenue of the Americas
4th and 5th Floors
New York, NY 10104

Distributed in Canada by Canadian Manda Group
664 Annette St., Toronto, Ontario, Canada M6S 2C8

ISBN 978 1 78472 418 4

A CIP catalogue record for this book is available from the
British Library.

Printed and bound in China

10 9 8 7 6 5 4

Publisher: Alison Starling
Senior Editor: Pollyanna Poulter
Copy Editor: Zia Mattocks
Art Director: Juliette Norsworthy
Designer: Ben Brannan
Picture Research Manager: Giulia Hetherington
Production Controller: Dasha Miller
Illustrator: Judith van den Hoek

Contents

Introduction:
Why Dress Like a Parisian?

Why are there *so many* books about French, and especially Parisian, style? Do we really have that mysterious "*je ne sais quoi*"?

Oui, we do! It doesn't mean we are the most stylish women in the world (OK, it kind of does…), but dressing "like a Parisian" is an actual *thing* that we cannot deny still exists in this globalized world where each town seems to have been conquered by the same big fashion brands.

Yet you don't need to be in Paris to dress like a Parisian and not all Parisians dress like one. Dressing like a Parisian is an attitude. It might be something you were born with, or something you learned. If you haven't yet, this book has been written for you.

Before we start the style lesson, let's look at seven key qualities that define Parisian style…

Aloïs

1. La Nonchalance
Effortlessnes

2. L'Élégance
Elegance

La Parisienne – famous, you may say, for her ability to ooze the "I woke up like this" effect.

I know what you are thinking…But to achieve an everyday Parisian style really *is* pretty easy. Throw on some perfect, basic clothes, stunning accessories and an optional statement piece, don't overdo your hair, apply a bold lipstick, and *voilà*!

The effort was made long ago when actually BUYING the clothes. The key is to invest time in finding the basics and statement clothes that are ideal for you, the most wonderful accessories, the lipstick shade that makes you glow and, as for the hair – well, we just aren't so keen on blow-drying and straightening (*oui*, lazy could be the appropriate word).

The fact that dressing like a Parisian can be achieved quickly doesn't mean we are always ready in a few seconds. *La Parisienne*, aiming to impress her peers with a more creative style, may change outfits several times before going to a cocktail party or dinner. We are creatures of contrasts.

Ultimately, she will still end up with a very natural, sophisticated style, making us all believe that it was so easy for her.

For *la Parisienne* there is never an excuse not to be elegant. The best recipe for always being elegant? Only own elegant clothes.

The good thing about elegance is that it is something you keep forever. Have you spotted the cute Parisian grandmas, dressed in tiny heels, earrings and a neat coat to pop down to the grocery store? Elegance is everyday visual politeness.

Yet please don't mistake elegance for conservative and boring. You *can* wear ripped jeans, a printed T-shirt, a spiked ear cuff, worn-out Converse AND still be elegant. It is all about the clothes you choose and your attitude when wearing them.

Visiting a foreign country and walking all day? Wear some beautiful stylish flats. Holidaying in the south of France where it is super-warm? Go for a pretty summer dress or denim shorts and sandals. Shopping at the Sunday morning market? No makeup (maybe just lipstick – it only takes a sec) and not much hairstyling (as usual) with a great-fitting pair of jeans and the perfectly cut Breton top that always hangs effortlessly in the closet.

3. La Discrétion
Understatement

The first words that come to mind when you think of Parisian style could be "effortless, chic and understated". Some may even say "boring".

I can't deny that most of our fashion icons, from yesterday's actresses to today's bloggers, built their style legend on perfectly chosen basics. BUT they were basics put together with a lot of attitude.

Others go for more daring options. But even when wearing the sexiest red party dress, *la Parisienne* is never "too much". She can thank the nonchalance of her attitude (and her lack of competence/laziness in all hair-and-makeup-related things) for tempering the boldness of her clothes.

In the end, isn't it supremely refined to be discreet in a world in which everyone tries to stand out?

4. La Sensualité
Sensuality

Aaaah, *les Parisiennes*…the most gorgeous women in the world, aren't we?

OK, OK, the rumours may be slightly exaggerated, but we are kind of sexy, aren't we? Despite the fact that we tend to have less obviously sexy clothes, hair and makeup than women in many other countries.

My in-depth analysis of the Parisian woman has led me to identify that "*le naturel*" is probably her most important secret. Our conception of beauty is to reveal what's already there rather than add to it or hide it. Therefore, we stay away from anything that could transform us too much, such as heavy makeup, overprocessed hairdos, plastic surgery, push-ups and so on.

We always stay in touch with our own sensuality, embracing our singularity and making it our best asset rather than trying to fit into a doll-like prescriptive formula.

5. Le Plaisir
Fun

La Parisienne enjoys dressing up as a way to express her creativity. The person she is looking to please the most with her outfits is herself.

She doesn't take fashion too seriously and trends do not really matter to her. I have noticed that my English and American clients often ask me what the shapes, colours and prints of the moment are, whereas my French clients never do. Yet *la Parisienne* may follow fashions when they please her and, as long as she likes them, doesn't care about wearing the same trendy sneakers as half of her co-workers.

If you asked *la Parisienne*, she would say she doesn't care much about rules either, as she is a free spirit. Truth is, they may be so ingrained in her DNA that she doesn't realize she is following them.

Even if it is full of dos and don'ts, the French style always contains a hint of wit and playfulness. *Oui*, to a funky print, a scarf in the hair or a vintage brooch.

"Be light-hearted and don't overthink it" would be her dressing mantra (if she were to have one).

6. *La Singularité*
Individuality

Each *Parisienne* dreams of having a "signature style" – and there are as many styles as there are *Parisiennes*: bohemian, rock chick, classic, glamorous, arty…

Yet, to be honest, our obsession with perfect basics may make us look alike. It is not unusual to meet up with a friend and discover that she, too, is wearing a striped top with jeans and stilettos, especially when you consider that lots of your friends will like the same things as you.

Nevertheless, *la Parisienne* dreams of being unique. For her, singularity lies in the details. When shopping for clothes, she looks for lesser-known brands, second-hand treasures or the hidden gems of the high street. Nothing makes her happier than revealing that her "cute little top" (in France, every cute piece of clothing can qualify as "petit") came from the flea market.

In the end, one out of two *Parisiennes* may own a trench coat but they will all wear it in a different way.

7. *La Rébellion*
Breaking the Rules

Be *Parisienne*, be free-spirited.

Everything you will read on the following pages consists of advice. Or, more accurately, style recipes that you can choose to follow or break away from.

My tips refer to a typical, stylish yet quite classic Parisian style. You could think of this book as being like a cookbook of French cuisine: all about French dressing (but with no vinaigrette in sight). As with all great cookbooks, I will give you "easy recipes", as well as some more advanced ones.

Some would argue that style is an art that shouldn't be limited by rules…What I will share with you in this book are not "rules" but more guidelines, styling tricks and inspirations for those who want to be more stylish and chic, *à la Parisienne*. Take a little time to read on and, who knows, hopefully by the end you will have finally mastered this "effortless" French look.

Chapter 1

Neutrals & Brights

The Parisian Approach to Couleur

There is a myth about us Parisians wearing only black. Coco Chanel may have invented the little black dress (*la petite robe noire*), and we are very grateful to her, but that is not an accurate view of all of us, all of the time (having said that, typing this on my laptop while wearing an all-black outfit makes me feel like something of a fraud).

It is true to say, however, that our favourite colours are neutrals. On a daily basis, each of our outfits tends to contain at least one. My definition of a neutral colour is one that doesn't conflict with any other. It is like an outfit's blank canvas. A neutral colour may be black, white, grey, beige or navy blue; or their variations, such as cream, sand, taupe and so on. I also consider natural leather and denim to be neutrals because they, too, match everything.

To be complete, a wardrobe needs many neutral-coloured pieces of clothing, each with the wonderful ability to be so versatile that you can create countless combinations with it. Owning a lot of neutral pieces makes your morning routine much easier because there will always be a good match for your most daring clothes. And neutrals all work together with each other, too.

But, of course, we also wear some "real" colours. Since we like to be discreet, subdued shades are our preference. For our main pieces, we often go for understated colours, such as a delicate rose, a stormy blue or an earthy green, rather than a fuchsia pink, an electric blue or a bright green, which we prefer to use as accents.

So first, let me walk you through the key neutrals and then we'll get reacquainted with colour and how to use it.

"A neutral is like an outfit's blank canvas... But, of course, we also wear some 'real' colours"

Black & Navy Blue

Black is the foundation of a Parisian's wardrobe. It has a reputation for always being elegant and matching everything, and it perfectly transitions from day to night. Yet there are many preconceived ideas about black that need to be debunked.

…"Black matches everything"
Not true. As black has a sophisticated, dressy feel, it does not work well with very summery prints or bright, fresh colours – with the exception of washed-out black jeans.

The darkest colour in the spectrum, black makes every other colour appear brighter. Therefore, when wearing a bold colour with black, it is a good idea to make either the black *or* the bold colour dominate, so that the contrast feels subtler. *Par exemple*:

• A black dress with yellow shoes = oh, *oui!*
• A yellow dress with black shoes = oh, *oui!*
• Black trousers with a yellow top = oh, *non*, far too bumble bee (dear bumble bees, please don't get upset).

…"Black equals elegant"
Unless worn stylishly, an all-black outfit will simply make you look invisible.

How to wear black
Pops of bright, warm colours, such as red, burgundy, rust, sunflower yellow and, of course, gold, will make black appear lively and elegant.

Avoid neon colours, which lack subtlety when contrasted with black.

Silver, greys and blues will give black a cool, urban look.

For larger pieces of clothing, go for dark colours that will create a subtle contrast and give the black item a sultry look, such as olive green, navy blue, burgundy, deep raspberry or burnt orange. Or try pastel and whitened shades, which will look less girly next to black.

Join the navy
If you feel black is too sophisticated or too harsh for you, think of replacing it with navy blue, its more polished, bourgeois brother. Unlike black, navy matches almost every colour and, being lighter, contrasts more subtly with bright hues.

**Must-have
blacks**

1. Flats
2. Heels
3. Bag
4. Tights (pantyhose)
5. Top
6. Sweater
7. Trousers
8. Skirt

*"Black and white
do not stand being
dirty or cheap"*

White

The purest of all colours, white is dangerous for a *Parisienne* who spends the day riding *le métro* or a *vélib* bike and lunching on salads with unruly leafs or *plats en sauce*. Yet for a fresh, natural, daytime glow, a white top is definitely worth the risk. White will also make you stand out at summer gatherings and evening cocktail parties (again, mind the sauce).

Pale and dusty shades
For a soft contrast, go for pale and dusty colours: a white T-shirt looks amazing with washed-out blue denims, a pale pink skirt or a grey jacket.

Warm neutrals
Make your whites shine by pairing them with items in delicate mother-of-pearl, champagne, silver or rose-gold shades.

Naturals
Khaki, beige or caramel leather are a forever friend of white.

Dark or muted shades
Avoid colours that are too saturated, such as a bold red or a neon yellow, and favour more understated, dark or muted shades.

White as a main
All-over white is fresh and pure. You can accessorize it with natural colours, and play with transparency and shapes. You can also choose white for a key piece, such as a top, blazer, trousers or coat (yet that last one is for princesses who only sit on clean spots).

White as a pop
Use white as a highlighter. Layering a white T-shirt or shirt underneath something is a great way to add lightness to an outfit. Imagine dark blue jeans with a dark green cashmere sweater…not bad, but it feels a bit sad. Now add a white shirt underneath your sweater, let the sleeves, collar and hem show and, *voilà*, you have a completely different outfit, where each piece stands out against the punctuation of the white shirt.

Must-have whites
- Lots of white tops (T-shirts, shirts…)
- White denim jeans
- A white summer dress

Beige & Nude

I call these shades warm neutrals, as opposed to the cold neutrals of grey or navy blue. As it resembles skin (from pale to dark tones), beige matches pretty much everything. Nude has the same effect in an exaggerated manner.

Choose a shade that works best with your skin tone but beware: worn close to the face, these colours may make your complexion look dull. I recommend you compensate for this with lively makeup and striking accessories.

Beige and nude are usually considered daytime colours, but they can be used for eveningwear if the fabric is shiny.

Must-have beige items

- Trench coat
- Warm wool or cashmere top
- Camisole

What to match with beige and nude

- Soft colours

Just like white, beige and nude work well with soft, subtle shades, including white.

- Warm colours

Beige and nude are a sultry match for warm shades, such as brown, red, burgundy and yellow.

- Dark colours

These neutrals pair well with dark shades, such as forest green, plum and burnt orange. They can also make black look more casual (the little black dress with a beige trench coat, for example), but can look too conservative with navy blue.

- Flashy colours

Beige and nude are the ultimate shades to use to help soften super-bold, flashy or neon colours.

Grey

Grey has a cool, urban feel, making it the perfect choice for at least pretending that you are a very professional individual. It's best suited to daytime but if you want to take it on a night out, pimp it up like Cinderella and transform it into silver (I promise you won't turn into a pumpkin at midnight).

What to match with grey

• Soft colours
Treated as a neutral, grey is your best shot for making pastels and pale, soft colours look edgy.
• Dark colours
Grey looks good with black and/or cold blues, topped with silver accessories.
• Bright colours
Grey also works well with vitamin-loaded bold shades, such as tangerine, sunshine yellow, bright red or Barbie pink.

Useful grey items

• T-shirts
• Cashmere or wool sweaters
• Blazer

Twist your neutrals

Good news: all of the key neutrals that I have listed on the previous pages will work together. You *can* wear dark blue cigarette trousers, a white shirt, a beige trench coat and black accessories all at the same time.

However, wearing only neutral colours can sometimes look boring. *Pas de panique, mesdames*, there is an easy cure for colour depression: spice up your neutrals with pops of bright colours. Red, prints, metallic shades and anything that catches the light are must-have remedies.

Bright pops to boost your neutrals

• Lipstick
• Nail polish
• Shoes
• Bag
• Scarf
• Gloves
• Hat
• Jewellery

Getting to Know *Couleur*

While most *Parisiennes* do not have a very colourful wardrobe, some seem to have a sixth sense when it comes to matching colours. Good news, this magic can be deciphered through the colour wheel (*see* below), which contains all the colours in the light spectrum: the primary, the secondary, the tertiary and as many as the wheel designer wants to represent.

It is worth remembering that the colour wheel shows only the most intense shades. It does not show darker or lighter versions, such as midnight blue or baby blue.

In order to mix colours creatively, remember that a colour can be determined by two essential parameters:

Hue: The name the colour goes by – blue, green, turquoise…They are infinite.

Intensity: The darkness or lightness of a colour. For subtle colour mixes, I suggest you use more of the less intense shades and less of the bright ones.

Note that the colour-matching tricks in this chapter will work with any variation of the hue in terms of intensity.

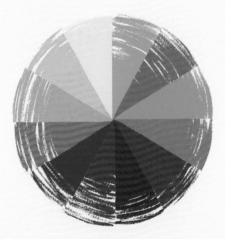

"Some Parisians seem to have a sixth sense when it comes to matching colours"

The classics and beyond

When you think "colours", there are a
few classics that always come to mind.
The neutrals – very much appreciated
by *la Parisienne,* as we have already seen.
The primary "bold" colours – less popular
with *les Parisiennes,* with the exception of
red (*see* pages 32–3) and mostly used as
"pops". The pastels (*see* page 31) – basically
a whiter version of a colour...And myriad
complex shades you can't even name.

But unnameable does not equal unwearable.
In fact, the more complicated the shade is
to describe, the more interesting it is to wear
(this, *ma chérie,* is a dove, stormy, pale blue...
par exemple). It means there has been a colour
designer behind the scenes, researching
what new hue he or she could create for
an unexpected result.

Couleur caution

• In fast fashion you find too many "ready-
made" colours that are harsh on the
complexion (see that flashy turquoise, cheap
polyester top on the shelf? Don't go there).
• Bold and saturated hues work best in a
quality fabric and in a shade that flatters
your complexion.

Safe and stylish

To look different and stylish, I recommend
you select main colours that are:
• Either pale or dark
• In-between hues (such as yellow-orange,
violet-blue)
• Muted and not very intense colours – these
can be easier to pair because their contrasts
are softer, so you do not have to worry too
much about violent colour clashes or colour
overload. (*See also* tips on page 28.)

Complementary *Couleurs*

Complementary colours enhance each other's characteristics while balancing them.

Opposites attract

Look at opposite sides of the colour wheel to discover which colours complement each other. You feel your dark blue outfit has a cold and sad feel? Throw on a pair of warm-orange leather boots and, bam, the energy is back. Some of the complementary colour mixes are all-time classics, such as the red and green of typical Scottish plaid (hi Santa) or Seventies orange with purple. And don't forget to read between the lines: blue-green looks wonderful with red-orange.

Nextdoor styling

If you are looking for more discreet matches, you can opt for neighbouring colours. These are placed next to each other on the colour wheel – green and blue, for example, or red and orange. Looking for something a little more daring? Match with the next-door-but-one colour on the wheel. For instance, blue looks great with yellow, and green is amazing with violet.

Staying subtle

Pairing blocks of intense colours could lead to retina saturation…definitely something that *la Parisienne* would disapprove of.

Colour blocking tips

• Add pops of one colour
A blue dress with orange earrings, perhaps.

• Position brights away from each other
Red shoes and a green sweater will be softened by blue jeans and a classic beige trench coat.

• Choose subdued shades
An orange skirt with either a dark purple top or a pale lilac one, instead of plain, intense purple.

• If you must colour block with intense shades…
try neighbouring colours: red and purple or red and orange will definitely make you stand out… but this is not very French, *ma chérie*.

Pastels

Pastels are soft, pale colours. If you were a painter, you would add white to your palette in order to create them.

Pastels are spontaneously associated with innocence and sweetness, and wearing them as a grown-up can be tricky when you are into "low-sugar" fashion. If you are aiming for a less sweet result, you can go for dusty, greyish or whitened pastel shades.

What to match with pastels

Main matches

- **Pale neutrals**
  White, grey, beige and nude are the perfect companions to pastels.

- **Other pastels**
  The softness of pastel shades gives them the ability to all work together. Of course, the complementary or the neighbouring colour matches still work when using pastels.

- **Jeans**
  Because jeans make everything soft look cool rather than girly.

Accent matches

- **Black**
  Black accessories make a pastel outfit look more edgy.

- **Bright red**
  It'll liven up any pastel outfit. Pops of lemon yellow would also work – for instance, with lilac or blue.

- **Leopard print**
  This won't work with every shade but, yes, indeed, try it with baby yellow or blue.

"Wearing pastels can be tricky when you are into 'low-sugar' fashion"

Bright Red

As the quintessential sensual colour, bright red is a Parisian's most beloved accent. It is the magic wand that can turn a so-so outfit into something stylish and full of energy.

Good news, you can use bright red as an accent to almost everything as it is an easy colour to match. Choose your perfect shade according to your complexion, your mood that day or the other colours you are wearing. The reds that contain yellow feel like a burning flame, while pinkish reds feel fresh, and reds that contain blue feel more sophisticated.

Favourite bright red accents
- Lipstick
- Nail polish
- Shoes
- Bag
- Print detail
- Delicate jewellery

Favourite red mixes

Soft neutrals
Grey, beige and camel always work with bold shades worn as a main piece by softening their intensity with subtle contrast. Picture a little red dress with a beige trench coat; isn't it adorable?

Black
When mixing red with black, I suggest you go for one of them as a main colour and use the other as an accent. Also, stay away from cheap fabrics and, I promise, you won't look like a costume witch. A red dress with black shoes and bag – simple and efficient.

White
This is a way to get your red to look fresh and innocent, *à la Brigitte Bardot*. Picture a red skirt worn with a white T-shirt. Or white cropped jeans worn with red espadrilles.

Black-and-white print
A print is a subtle addition that can complement a black-and-red mix as a third element. Think of black-and-white gingham mini shorts and a red sweater with black tights (pantyhose) and shoes.

Pink
Whether it is a soft or a bold shade, this neighbouring colour is always a great pairing. What about a red mini skirt worn with a pink T-shirt?

Burgundy
Pairing red with burgundy involves using the *camaïeu* trick (*see* page 35) of matching two colours that are very similar to one another, which always works wonders. Imagine wearing your sultry bold red maxi skirt with a burgundy camisole.

Pastels

I recommend using the pastel as a main colour and red as an accent. The red will take away the sweetness of the pale shade and energize it.

Khaki

An earthy khaki is the perfect rough contrast to sexy bright red. Picture an oversize military jacket on a vampy red mini dress.

Blue

Red and blue is an all-time classic (the French flag has been sporting this combo successfully for a while), which works no matter what the shade of blue. How about wearing your jeans with red boots and a white tee?

Prints

If you want to soften red, use it in a print – narrow red-and-white candy-cane stripes, red flowers on a black background, a striped red and navy blue Breton top…

Style tip: A mix of red and white in equal proportions may lack subtlety. Instead, use either one of the colours as a main and the other as a detail. A white shirt dress with red lips and nails, for example. Or a white shirt popping out from underneath a red sweater. You can also achieve a subtle look with a piece that contains some of the other colour, such as a red skirt with white polka dots worn with a white camisole.

Camaïeu & Monochrome

Wearing the same colour from head to toe, also known as monochrome, can easily make you look as though you have no style at all if it is poorly done.

Camaïeu

French for "different shades of a colour", *camaïeu* is a very stylish and subtle play on monochrome. The variation from one shade to another could be caused by a difference in hue or a difference in intensity. You can also vary one or both.

- *Camaïeu* **as a complete outfit:** such as head-to-toe yellow hues, from pale to dark.
- *Camaïeu* **on parts of your outfit:** such as a pale yellow top, dark yellow boots and bright yellow-framed glasses with light blue jeans and a beige trench coat.

Monochrome

Although black monochrome is a *Parisienne*'s favourite, you could go monochrome with every colour, as long as you have the perfect match in your closet. Dark shades are by far the easiest to pull off. A bold colour match of a dress, shoes and makeup is a daring choice for a special event, whereas a monochrome look in a soft neutral can be elegant and delicate…but beware of looking dull.

Tips for a stylish black monochrome

Play on textures
Smooth black jeans with a smooth sweater? *Pffff.* Boring. Raw-cotton black jeans with a fluffy sweater? *Oui, merci.*

Play on shine
A play on texture practically equals playing with shine. Each fabric has a different way of reflecting the light. Think as if you were the French master of black, the artist Pierre Soulages, and balance matte and shiny, opaque and sheer.

Go for perfect cuts
Without colour, the only thing you'll pay attention to is the silhouette. Make it sharp, make it loose, make it simple or sophisticated but, most important, make it perfectly balanced.

Choose quality fabrics
Black can't stand a cheap shiny polyester fabric. Go for silk, beautiful cotton, denim or high-end synthetics.

Accessorize
Add a hint of gold or silver jewellery, either large or small, to catch the light.

Do an "almostochrome"
Wear one or two accessories, such as shoes, lipstick or gloves, in a contrasting colour. Red or gold shoes with a black jumpsuit, for instance. You can also go for subtler options that create a less obvious contrast. A mono such as burgundy with navy blue, or yellow with nude.

Ditch the *Trois-Couleur* Rule

Popular opinion has a lot to say about fashion. Red does not suit blondes; do not mix black and navy; gold and silver don't match; and, above all, DO NOT WEAR MORE THAN THREE COLOURS IN AN OUTFIT. Otherwise, you'll look like a clown or a parrot (oooh, frightening).

Absurdité, I say. You CAN wear more than three colours in an outfit as long as you choose them wisely. And here is how:

Temper the brights

Three is a good maximum number when it comes to bright colours.

If you wear several bright colours, wear one as a main and the others as accents. Or, wear all of them as accents. It is better to wear little flashes of bright colours rather than big colour blocks next to each other. For instance, a bright red sweater with light blue jeans and fuchsia shoes. Or a white T-shirt with blue jeans and a trench coat, together with a bright red belt and fuchsia shoes.

Wear low-intensity shades

Such as muted or pastel tones, which are easier to match as they are less flashy.

Include some neutrals

Aaaah, neutrals…the secret style weapon of *la Parisienne* when it comes to wearing colour. Including some neutrals in an outfit is a good way to wear lots of colours while staying elegant.

For instance, if you are wearing a light blue top with a bright green skirt and baby pink nails, match them with cream Converse and a beige trench coat.

Use *camaïeu* (see page 35)

Because several shades of the same colour feel like one colour. Picture a washed-out blue top with an electric blue belt, soft blue jeans and midnight blue boots.

Embrace prints

Prints themselves can be proof that the three-colour rule is not a rule because they frequently contain more colours. Wearing a print often means you are instantly breaking the rule…for the better.

Equations to remember

Three brights alone is too much

One bright green vest
+
one bright yellow blouse
+
one red skirt
=
hello clown

Even though you DID respect the "rule".

However:

Three brights with neutrals works

One bright green bag
+
bright yellow shoes
+
bright red lipstick and nail polish
+
pale blue jeans
+
one white blouse
=
classy

Even though you are actually wearing the tremendous amount of five colours (*oh là là*).

Don't Be Matchy Matchy

Our grandmothers took great care in matching the details of their outfits, which was considered super-elegant. Nowadays, this manner of assembling clothes feels like you are "trying too hard". We all know that dressing like a *Parisienne* is about looking effortless. But does this mean that matching colours is totally over?

Not at all. But there is such a thing as being too matchy. I would define "too matchy" as being "when the match is really obvious". For example, matching the same bright colour, which contrasts strongly with the rest of the outfit, on at least two noticeable pieces of clothing located far apart from each other.

Style tips:
• The more items you match, the more likely you are to be too matchy (at least, until you reach monochrome, *see* page 35). A turquoise bag, turquoise shoes, turquoise nails…Overdose!
• Avoid the sandwich effect, also called the bee effect (both named by me) – a layer of red shoes, a layer of black trousers, a layer of an identical red top, a layer of black blazer, a layer of perfectly matching red lipstick…Stop, stop!

How to match without being too matchy

• **Match your print's minor colour with another item**
You have a red-dotted blouse? Match the dots with your red bag.

• **Match your makeup with your clothes**
Try red lips with the aforementioned red-dotted blouse.

• **Match jewellery with your clothes**
But not all of it. Simply the red earrings with the red-dotted blouse.

• **Match pieces that are close to each other**
A red belt or bag with a red-dotted top, for instance, instead of a red bag with red shoes, which are located further apart from each other in the outfit.

• **Match less saturated colours, such as darker or paler shades**
For instance, matching burgundy shoes and a burgundy belt is a less obvious match than red shoes and a red belt.

• **Match neutrals**
If you match white, black or beige items, it'll go unnoticed. A black bag with black shoes? What's more commonplace?

• **Match similar shades**
Matching pink shoes and a pink bag with a black outfit is very noticeable because of the strong contrast between pink and black. The effect would be much more discreet in an outfit containing all shades of pink.

Shine On

Parisian I may be but I am convinced that I have glitter in my veins. And, no, shine is not technically a colour but still…

A little or a lot of shine will make an outfit stand out, whether for day- or night-time. This explains why *les Parisiennes* love it and wear shiny items wherever they are going and whatever time it is.

With all things better in moderation, as we say about wine (well, as the French Ministry of Health says), I recommend that you start with one shiny item. It could be anything – shoes, trousers, a top, a bag…And be creative. And do not limit yourself to gold and silver. What about dark blue sequins or pink metallics? And, hey, sometimes you can drink more wine than recommended… or wear more glitz when night falls.

Where to shine
• Lurex (clothes)
• Sequins (clothes)
• Glitter (glued onto clothes or as makeup)
• Metallics (clothes or makeup)

Daytime shine
• Details are best for daytime: a pair of shiny socks, metallic shoes, a silver eyeliner…
• Lurex and metallics feel less like they belong to a party than sequins and glitter.
• Make casual or classic pieces sparkle. A square sweater will always have a daytime look, no matter its marvellous silver shade.
• Feeling confident? Try a strong, shimmery piece, such as a metallic skirt or a Lurex top.
• Balance shiny items with understated basics: gold brogues with cigarette trousers and a blazer for the office; a Lurex cardigan over jeans and a white T-shirt at the weekend.
• Master cool-casual daytime glitz by pairing a band T-shirt with a silver mini skirt; jeans with a sparkly, striped Breton top, a gold shirt under a trench coat.

Night-time shine
When the stars come out, you can either abide by the "understated" rules, above, or you can dare to wear a shiny statement item (dress, blazer, top…). "Impossible is not French," as we say, yet there are a few tricks to master to avoid looking too disco ball:
• One sparkly item is enough, makeup and accessories included.
• Wear very little jewellery.
• Avoid doll-like makeup and hair.
• Try mixing several metallic shades, such as copper and dark blue, or silver and pink.

Chapter 2

Prints

The Parisian Approach to Prints

I am guessing that the second you read this title you thought about horizontal stripes. They are so iconic that Parisian caricatures often depict men and women in a Breton striped top and a beret, holding a baguette.

I must admit, this is not that far-fetched… There have been countless times I have met up with friends – male and female – and several of us have been sporting the same classic lines on our *"marinières"*.

That said, you do not need prints to dress like a Parisian. As we discussed in the introduction, a classic Parisian wardrobe consists of basics, thoughtfully accessorized.

" Prints may be considered a wardrobe basic or a statement piece"

But here's where the lines blur…Prints may be considered a wardrobe basic or an accessory/statement piece. For instance, classic-coloured stripes in, say, navy or black are so timeless that they don't make your top any less of a basic. In neutral colours, stripes match pretty much everything, in the same way as a plain top would. They just help spice up your staples.

More daring prints definitely enter the accessory/statement piece category. They really stand out and won't match everything. *Les Parisiennes* would wear them on small items – such as scarves (Hermès or others), bags or shoes – or on basic items, transforming them into designer pieces: a shirt, a pair of jeans or a kimono can look outstanding in the right print. The not-in-the-fashion-industry *Parisienne* usually won't wear more than one print per outfit, but the style pro will mix them.

Last but not least, there is a print for everyone, no matter their shape, so don't stay away from prints for the wrong reasons.

Choose Your Print

Just like colour accents, prints are an easy way to break up the monotony of a plain-coloured outfit. When choosing a print, you have two options:

1. Go bold: by using crazy prints on a large amount of fabric.
2. Remain discreet: by using either understated prints or bold ones but in moderation.

Daring prints

Perfect worn on an accessory as a lively pop, or on a large piece to make a statement…
I would qualify "daring" prints as those that feature more than one of the following:
• Bold colours
• Large patterns
• Contrasting patterns

Bold colours with small contrasting patterns work wonders on small accessories such as shoes and bags. For instance: bright flower-print shoes, a coloured snake-print bag or a batik-print headband (for more on batik prints *see* page 67).

Large, contrasting patterns work better on large pieces, such as a shirt, a kimono, a blazer, a dress, a wide skirt or a coat.

Think of non-repeating large patterns for scarves: this way, your scarf will look different each time you tie it.

Discreet prints

As you probably guessed, these are the prints that do not feature the characteristics that constitute a daring print.

Prints with two neutral colours are still considered a neutral and can therefore work well with any bold colour. Think black and white, navy and cream and shades of grey. Use them to make large pieces more interesting while remaining easy to wear. Great on: sweaters, cardigans, coats, shirts, tops and so on.

Prints with a very mild contrast act more like a textured fabric than an actual print. Picture tiny gold dots on a beige shirt or a navy blue and black plaid coat. They are discreet, yet they make your piece look interesting, and they remain easy to match because you can consider this *camaïeu* print (*see* page 35) as a single colour.

Harmonize Your Print

If you wear a print next to a plain colour, it can either stand out or blend into your outfit. If you want to go for the second option, you should use a transition colour between the print and the other items you are wearing by having one of the colours contained in the print for the plain fabric next to it.

A wide variety of prints feature a background and a detail colour. In some cases it can be smart to pick out the detail colour as a match, whereas in others the background would be a better choice.

Detail colour print transition

Let's imagine you own a printed dress that features large bright pink and red flowers on a navy blue background. You are looking for a cardigan to match because it has become a bit chilly. A clever choice would be to select a cardigan in one of the flower colours – either red or pink or a flowery neighbouring shade of them. You could also choose those detail print colours for accessories such as a belt, bag, shoes or nails (yes, I consider makeup an accessory).

Background colour print transition

A navy blue cardigan would have also worked wonders with the aforementioned little dress, for a more understated result.

Dominated or dominant colour transition

I call the dominant colour the bolder one. Generally, the dominant colour is the detail colour, while the dominated colour is the background colour. This is the case for the previously mentioned printed dress, where pink and red are dominating navy blue.

Matching with the dominant colour can feel overwhelming, especially if it is also the background colour. For instance, a bright green top printed with black stars will be better matched with a black leather skirt than with a green one. However, a black top with bright green stars could be matched with a bright green leather skirt.

You do not have a dominant colour if both are of equal strength, such as on a Breton striped top where navy blue and white are both considered neutrals.

When not to harmonize

Sometimes matching can be counterproductive…

Base layer matching

Matching the base (the layer worn underneath the print) with the printed layer will, most of the time, wash it out. When in doubt, opt for a base in contrasting white, which will make your printed layers radiant.

Blended prints matching

When your print is blended, and you cannot really distinguish the individual colours (as in a Liberty print or any other super-busy print), you should choose a neutral or contrasting shade to go with it, rather than one contained in the mix; otherwise the print won't stand out and you may end up with a pretty dull result. Imagine a Liberty-print shirt in fresh coral, pink, yellow and green shades. Wearing it with pale blue jeans will enhance its colours, whereas matching it with one of the aforementioned shades would make your outfit lack depth.

This advice does not apply when matching a top layer: you could wear your printed Liberty shirt with dark blue jeans AND a coral blazer.

Contrast Your Print

Sometimes, matching the print with a colour it already contains may wash it out or lead to an overwhelming result. To avoid this you can choose to add another plain colour to your outfit.

Contrasting neutral prints

If your print contains only neutral colours, you can match it with any other shade. For example, a black-and-white gingham print with red shoes and a beige trench coat. Or beige-and-cream striped trousers with a mustard-coloured shirt.

Contrasting coloured prints

Neutrals are always a good option. You can wear them as a base to make a coloured print look more vivid or as a layer to soften its intensity.

For instance, a white T-shirt under a floral-print kimono will make it glow, whereas a beige trench coat over a busy flowery dress will make it look more conservative.

You can also choose to wear a contrasting or a neighbouring colour with your print. Let's say your print is a *camaïeu* of orange: blue seems like a perfectly appropriate matching option.

Now, if your print contains two contrasting colours, such as pink and red flowers on a navy blue background, as we cited on page 48, you could choose to go with something that contrasts with the background colours, such as a shade of yellow, or with something that contrasts with one of the detail colours, such as a shade of green.

If your outfit contains one neutral colour and one bold colour in equal amounts, contrast the bold colour: a candy-cane red-and-white striped shirt with dark blue jeans, for example.

The contrasting or neighbouring colour match can be achieved with large pieces as well as accessories. For instance, you could wear your blue-and-white gingham with a bright yellow bag or shoes.

Mix Prints Together

First, remember that the easiest way to wear prints is not to mix them with others. That said, if you wish to be featured in the style pages of a magazine one day, or if you just enjoy taking a risk and looking awesome, you can try the following.

Think harmony
• Mix prints featuring the same colours.
• Mix prints that have a colour in common.
• Mix neutral-coloured prints with bold-coloured prints.
• Mix prints with complementary or neighbouring colours.

Play with pattern sizes
• Contrast small and large, dense and sparse.

Combine pattern shapes
• Mix similar patterns in different hues.
• Mix clashing patterns.

The geometry of stripes and the unruliness of flowers, along with similar unexpected mixes, are something I will develop later in the book (*see* pages 56–7 and 62–3).

Tips
• Big prints can make the body appear wider than it is.
• Prints containing contrasting colours are trickier to match than prints containing similar colours.

Anaïs Dautais Warmel

Age 30, founder of Les Récupérables, a brand that makes new clothes from vintage garments

I meet Anaïs in her cute sixth-floor apartment located in the charming village-like twentieth arrondissement. As I look around, the dark wood on the floor, the ladder used as a shelf, the piano, the plants, the iron balcony, everything feels homey and so typically Parisian.

How would you describe your style?
I'd say retro modern. Colourful, but not excessively so. Subtly sophisticated while letting my personality show.

Did it evolve?
Yes! Before, I was more eccentric, wearing acid colours and having bleached hair.

What's your style history?
I have been creating outfits ever since I was two years old. My mum would show me things in stores and I would choose one of them. I knew what I wanted. Especially when it came to colours and prints. After college I started working in thrift stores, doing the merchandising and styling the clients. Then I started to alter the clothes, and to create new ones, which led me to create my own brand, making clothes from recycled garments.

Could you share some style tricks?
• Never use more than three non-neutral colours together.
• Wide plus wide, you go West (in French: "*large sur large on prend le large*", which sounds better).
• When you wear a statement piece that is not an accessory, such as a printed jacket, build your look around it.

Do you have an iconic piece in your closet?
Way too many. I'd say my beloved flower-printed polyester kimono, though. It's mainly prints that determine my likes and dislikes.

Do you follow trends?
I tend to avoid trends, but in the end, I am trendy. It would actually be more accurate to say that I don't pay attention to trends, especially anything that is mainstream. What I value the most is to look like no one else on the street.

What about makeup?
I can't go without a bit of red on the lips, some concealer for dark circles and highlighter for a healthy glow. Plus mascara, of course.

How would you describe French style?
Not tacky. It is all about "*le chic de la Parisienne*". I can find it deadly boring when it is too bourgeois, too conventional. I value the fact that fashion is always here to enhance the beauty of the wearer and is not just dedicated to making the clothing or makeup industries more profitable. For me, Jane Birkin is the iconic *Parisienne*. Just like her, *la Parisienne* is intrinsically stylish.

Stripes

Stripes are probably the most casual and easiest to wear of all prints. Whether vertical or horizontal, they spice up any outfit while matching pretty much everything. Ultimate bonus points: the horizontal ones guarantee you'll be mistaken for a French person.

Choosing

Medium-width contrasting stripes will be noticed while remaining casual.

For a textured effect, opt for ultra-thin stripes with low contrast, or stripes that shine.

Thick stripes are a bolder choice and, as a statement print, are less easy to match.

Neutral mixes are popular. Horizontally, the classic among classics is the Breton striped top in navy blue and white. Vertically, the classic blue-and-white striped shirt is a sharper way to wear stripes and a chic alternative to the white office staple.

You can also add colour to your stripes: a colour and white, a colour and a neutral, two-colours and even multicoloured stripes. There are no limits.

Positioning

Striped tops are a must, as the star of the show or as a base layer. A Breton top beneath a suede bomber jacket, perhaps, or the collar, cuffs and hem of a striped shirt peeking out from beneath a grey cashmere knit.

Vertically striped trousers are a classy option, whether narrow or wide stripes. A vertically striped skirt can also be an excellent choice.

Horizontal stripes are tricky on the bottom half, although less so if they are part of a dress. Avoid if you do not wish to increase the apparent width of your hips.

Stripes on accessories should be noticeable. Yes to a big, striped scarf, Gryffindor (or Slytherin) style.

Mixing

Unruly prints
As a geometrical print, stripes do very well with unruly prints, which include:
- Floral prints
- Leopard print
- Batik print

Dots
Stripes also work well with another essential geometrical print, dots (*see* pages 58–9).

Graphic prints
Try stripes with band or touristy T-shirts (*see* pages 68–9).

Plaid
A riskier choice but sometimes successful, you can try combining stripes with plaids (*see* pages 64–5).

Dots

The most adorable of all prints. When I think dots, I imagine a beautiful woman wearing her prettiest dotted dress to attend the *bal du 14 juillet* in her native village. Totally *une image d'Epinal* (an idyllic image). Dots, no matter their size and colour, always have a fresh, innocent, feminine and festive feel about them. Although I just wrote "feminine", I can totally picture an elegant gentleman wearing a dotted shirt or narrow scarf. So dots can ALSO have something dandy and androgynous about them.

Choosing

The classic of classics would be white dots on black – perfect on a flowing cinched dress or just a top, if you are aiming to seduce a fireman on *la fête nationale*.

On dresses
• You could change the white into red.
• The size of those dots could go from tiny to medium.

On tops and sweaters
• You can dare to wear bigger dots.
• And go more crazy with the colours.
• Why not try multicoloured dots?
• And maybe a white, cream or navy blue background colour?

Tip: Like all large prints, large dots tend to enlarge the silhouette.

Positioning

In addition to dresses and tops, dots work well elsewhere, too.

Skirts, whether short or long, flowy or structured, are an excellent place for a dotted print.

Trousers are trickier, but you can go dandy with a tie-like print – such as a burgundy background with tiny cream dots – which looks great on narrow cigarette trousers or high-waisted oversize trousers.

Dots also look darling on accessories: a printed scarf, a hair band, a tiny polka-dot clutch, little socks peeking out from your loafers…

Mixing

Unruly prints
Being a geometrical print, dots will look cute with unruly prints such as floral or animal prints.

Stripes
A dotted print works well with its geometrical counterpart: stripes.

Hosiery
In winter, wear sheer black dotted plumetis tights (pantyhose) with pretty much everything. As they are only one colour, they are easy to mix yet still have a certain sassiness to them. What could be better? If you feel you are too old (or too serious) for polka-dot tights (pantyhose), why not try the sheer sock version, or even sparkly, coloured ones, to show between your cropped trousers and under-the-ankle shoes.

Leopard Prints

Parisian women like to be sexy, which is probably why they love leopard prints so much. Yet their biggest fear is to look like "*une cagole*" (a woman from the south of France who likes a little too much of most things: too much tan, too much hair bleach, too much skin on show, too-high heels, too much leopard print…you get the picture). In order not to leopardize (erm, jeopardize), their elegance, Parisian women are all about *dédramatiser* the leopard print (playing down the drama of the print).

Choosing

A sharp eye is the only hunting skill required to capture this timeless print. We're talking small black and brown spots on a camel-coloured background. Stand still in the store, browse the shelves, and, once you've caught your prey, examine it with caution.

As in nature, its spots should have softened edges and the print should be neither too large nor too small.

Animal fabrics (*faux* ones being totally appropriate), such as leather and fur, suit it best. Natural fabrics, such as cotton, linen and wool, also work. Avoid shiny synthetic fabric or anything too transparent.

The shape of the piece must be rather basic, even minimalist, so avoid ruffles and superfluous details.

Positioning

Start with accessories. A satchel, a belt, pumps…Then, when you feel confident, go for a statement piece.

Androgynous pieces are safe choices. A timeless leopard-print shirt could become one of your wardrobe staples. Narrow-legged cigarette trousers are a chic option. And a leopard-print blazer will make you look like a star.

You may even try skinny jeans for a rock-star vibe.

Avoid anything too feminine. Be cautious with leopard dresses, skirts and anything that contains flounces or is too tight.

Mixing

Beige
This conservative colour will always minimize a daring choice. Trench it up and you're good to go.

Navy blue
Another conservative colour that will have a similar effect to beige. What could go wrong with navy blue cigarette trousers?

White
The freshness of white works well with the wildness of leopard. White jeans are my favourite, but choose quality jeans to keep it looking classy.

Pastels
A great way to give girly a rock edge. Alexa Chung, the most Parisian of Londoners, was once spotted wearing a soft-yellow knit with a leopard-print mini skirt and classic black loafers – super-cool!

Dark colours
This mix can look overwhelming, so use as an accessory here: a leopard-print clutch with a dark green dress, for instance.

Black
Leopard print and black can look rock… but it can also look tacky. Select your clothes wisely.

Bold colours
Wearing bold colours next to a leopard print may look too much. Instead, try wearing them at a distance with neutrals in between, such as a leopard-print shirt, raw blue jeans, bold red boots and a trench coat.

Florals

Every bouquet is different and so are floral prints. You could look like a round, stiff, old-fashioned bouquet, or you can look like a vibrant bunch of fresh flowers, gathered in the forest. You could even look like the super-fashionable succulent mix displayed on your cool neighbour's wall. The trick is to choose your floral print wisely…You wouldn't want to look like a synthetic bouquet, would you?

"Flowers can be planted anywhere… The trick is to choose your print wisely"

Choosing

Avoid fabrics that look synthetic. Shiny polyesters do not make for flattering flowers.

Small and easy

An all-over floral with no space between the flowers creates a hue in which the pattern is almost indiscernible. This flatters everyone and has a fresh, innocent feel to it.

Prints featuring small, spaced-out flowers feel even more innocent and may resemble pyjama prints. They, too, are adorable and easy to wear. But beware of the colours you choose.

Big and daring

These prints are more risky. If their design is classic, they may have an old-fashioned feel. Nonetheless, they are a statement that can work on large pieces such as a kimono, dress or maxi skirt.

Colours

Floral prints are usually associated with pastel, soft or fresh colours (which makes sense since they feature flowers). If this feels a bit too *Little House on the Prairie* for you, then consider dark-coloured florals. Fresh flowers on a black background, for example, or a mix of dark roses. It looks much more rock or goth than naïve.

Positioning

Flowers can be planted anywhere.

The iconic piece would be a summer dress: flowing for weekends, more structured for work. This piece will save you on warm summer days when you lack inspiration.

Not a fan of the conventional? Invest in other floral pieces: trousers, shorts, a blazer, bomber jacket or kimono.

Of course, skirts and shirts are also perfect for this print.

For accessories, I recommend scarves with large flowers. Tiny flowers around the neck have a kind of pyjama feel. Floral prints are also an option for shoes and bags, but usually they do not work so well on leather and are not very versatile items.

Mixing

Plain colours

The easy way: match the colour to one featured in your print or go for a neutral.

Denim

Whatever its colour, denim gives florals an edge. The older the jeans are, the better the contrast.

Leather

Choose black for a girly rock style; natural for a gentlewoman vibe.

Stripes

The regularity of stripes complements the irregularity of flowers. They work wonders worn side by side or mixed in a single print.

Other prints

Floral prints also look great with animal prints such as leopard, zebra or cow. Flowers on flowers can work but are tricky: so try different scales and similar colours.

Plaids

There are many ways to cope with cold weather. Plaid is one of them, conveying something between gentlewomanly elegance and pure cosiness. Although strictly not the most French of prints, we Parisians definitely like to get our inspirations from all around the world.

Choosing

The key word is subtlety. A clumsy plaid will always make you look cheap. Therefore, I recommend you avoid harsh colour contrasts in the print. And, as usual, the fabric is important. Plaid doesn't print on polyester. Period.

Positioning

Trousers
They'll look amazing with a neutral top. You can choose either to underline their punk aura with black and sexy rock attire or play on their bourgeois side by mixing them with a crisp white shirt and a trench coat. Tight trousers will look more rock or officey, while wide ones will give you a sophisticated boho look.

Shirt
In a soft, delicate fabric, worn slightly unbuttoned at the neck, with rolled-up sleeves, a plaid shirt will look casually refined with leather trousers or dark jeans. If you like it more lumberjacky, choose a thick wool or cotton fabric and wear it either over a sexy top or dress or as stylish casual attire.

Blazer
A structured plaid blazer will add English sophistication to your outfits. It can be mixed with chic pieces such as cigarette trousers, more relaxed ones such as jeans, or sexy ones such as a short skirt. You could even go head-to-toe plaid with a full tuxedo.

Coat
Cosy and will make your everyday basic attire look super-stylish.

Skirt or dress
Straight, simple shapes look grown-up; pleated and short will look very Manga schoolgirl (which is cute).

Scarf
You can't go far wrong with this classic piece if it is thick and woolen. It can be regular size or very oversize – think small blanket (but not an actual blanket).

Mixing

Plain neutral colours
Plaid makes a statement, so there is no need to overload. White, black, navy and beige are safe choices – wear either one or two of these.

Hint of another colour
If your plaid contains a stripe in a dominant colour, choose another piece of clothing or accessory in this shade.

The basics
Jeans or black leather work with the casual look of plaid.

Busy prints…
such as leopard, can be overwhelming worn next to plaid, so leave some space between them, even if this is just a flash of ankle.

Less-busy prints…
such as plumetis tights (pantyhose), Breton stripes or a light flowery print work well with plaid.

Unusual Prints

Anything can become a print and so there are an endless number of them that cannot be classified. This is a good thing because, like unusual colours, unusual prints are statement items in themselves.

An unusual print could be in a classic style and colouring but with an unusual theme (planets, fish, toys…) or a classic theme with unusual colouring and/or positioning, such as fading-out flowers, rainbow stripes or both. All of which makes it totally impossible to establish any kind of rule for these prints but I strongly advise you to explore them because they really can up your style stakes and are less difficult to wear than you might think.

Some miscellaneous prints you can wear

Snake prints
Sexy and wild, snake print looks best on shoes and legs. It doesn't have to look realistic so don't rule out funky colours. Snake print looks amazing with white or black for a rock chick result. It is quite a versatile animal print and can be used on an accessory (such as a bag or shoes), which you can mix with other distant prints.

Naïve prints
Stars, lips, hearts, lobsters, cacti or whatever you could ever dream up as a tiny, spaced-out, all-over pattern. They make your look and your life more fun.

Batik prints
Typical African patterns that became fashion classics in the mid-Noughties. They consist of large geometrical prints and are usually brightly coloured. The fabric should be a heavy cotton cloth, which will wear well as a dress, skirt, top or headscarf (*à l'Africaine*). Wear batik prints with denim, under trench coats or with graphic-printed T-shirts.

Landscape prints
A picture printed on a piece of clothing. It could be a printed photo or a painting… the most important thing is that the print is an all-over pattern and has no repeat. These items are *soooo* statement that the safest way to wear them is to pair them with plain basics in neutral colours.

Graphic Tees

You already know that white and striped tees are among a Parisian's wardrobe essentials. But have you thought about graphic tees? You know, the ones with the name of your favourite band or brand, your university logo, a clever quote, the name of your dog, a cute rainbow or whatever else you fancy? They're certainly versatile and bring that touch of funky quirkiness we all love to any outfit. And there is no age limit for rocking the graphic tee. Once, browsing Pinterest, I encountered a very chic 60-something wearing a T-shirt that said, "Old is the new gold".

Choosing

To qualify as a graphic tee, the print should not be an all-over one but should be placed, usually, in the centre of the T-shirt, somewhere between the belly and the breasts. You can find them in cool stores, in random fast-fashion brands (yes, sometimes that's OK) or, if you prefer a vintage style, in thrift stores. A genuine, ironic wolves-howling-at-the-moon T-shirt is always preferable to a copy.

The background of the T-shirt can be any colour, as can the print. Logically, single-colour prints on plain backgrounds are easy to match, but so are multicoloured prints on neutral backgrounds. Don't overthink it; the graphic tee is a cheap item, so if you like it, go for it and you'll find a way to match it.

The print should somehow reflect your personality. It is a bit absurd to wear a band T-shirt if you have never heard of the group. I'm just preserving your street cred – you'll thank me later. But, hey, if the design is *reaaaally* cool…

You may want to avoid wearing a girl who is hotter than you on your tee. Also, be cautious about the message you are wearing – advertising "I am gorgeous" not only isn't very chic, but may also dismiss the fact that you are, indeed, gorgeous. You know, like when a brand's name contains the word "luxury": if it *was* luxurious, it wouldn't have to say so. The same goes for you.

Good news, there is no such thing as too many graphic tees in a wardrobe once you own the basics.

Mixing

The graphic tee has a fun, casual feel to it. Wear it with items of a similar style or use it to dress down items of different styles.

Denim

Any colour denim will work with a graphic tee. Opt for classic jeans, a mini skirt, mini shorts, a denim jacket...anything.

Something formal

Feeling like your mum in this pencil skirt? Add a band tee and a pair of sneakers.

Something sexy

Feeling too daring in this patent leather mini skirt? You know what the remedy is.

Something dressy

Feeling "too much" in this shiny, satin, pleated midi skirt? You guessed it.

Chapter 3

Shapes

The Parisian Approach to Shapes

The shape of clothing may reveal the personality of *la Parisienne* even more than the colour or print.

The shy ladies will opt for a reasonable width, depth and length in all things: clothes are never too loose or too tight, too short or too long…And bold ladies will go maxi. Mini skirts, oversize sweaters, floor-length dresses and flounces are her best friends.

Yet whatever her style, *la Parisienne* has a golden rule about shapes: balance. The most daring may wear the shortest skirt, but she'll balance it with a loose top, flat shoes or a masculine blazer.

"La Parisienne has a golden rule about shapes: balance"

Structure

What I call structured clothes are the ones made from a fabric stiff enough to be given a tailored structure. You can easily recognize such items in your closet: they need to be hung in order to maintain their shape.

Some examples of structured clothes
• Tailored cigarette trousers
• Blazer
• Peplum top

Unstructured clothes
On the flipside of structured clothes are voluminous, oversize items. I don't know about you, but when I think "oversize", the first two things that come to mind are:
• A teenager trying to hide her body.
• The *Vogue* editorial where the stick-thin model looks stunning in oversize outfits that would look like a potato sack on me (and not even a *Vogue* potato sack).

But in all things fashion there is hope. Introducing some structure will make your voluminous pieces more wearable so that you, too, can rock the oversize look.

Wear structured clothes with:

• **Other structured clothing for a powerful allure**
For instance: tailored cigarette trousers with a tailored blazer.

• **Loose clothes for a semi-casual edge**
For instance: tailored cigarette trousers with a loose camisole or a tailored blazer with a flowy maxi skirt.

• **Bodycon clothes for a sexy effect**
For instance: a bodycon knit tucked into a trapeze skirt. (For more on bodycon, *see* page 77.)

How to tame oversize clothes:

• **Match them with something skintight**
Such as a loose, oversize knit with a bodycon skirt.

• **Reveal some skin**
Wrists, ankles, décolletage, legs... separately or all at once.

• **Wear heels**
Especially when trying to pull off the full oversize look.

• **Add a belt**
It will reveal your true waist that is hidden somewhere under the oversize clothes.

• **Give it some shape**
Tuck the top in or layer something tighter over the top.

Bodycon

Stretchy cottons are tricky. They spare no detail of your body from public scrutiny and, at their worst, can appear cheap and see-through – a look to be avoided by even the firmest *physique*.

Thicker fabrics, stretchy or not, are good for bodycon bottoms or dresses. I like a tight dress in a thick cotton or a tight pencil skirt (with a side slit to enable walking) in a beautiful leather. There are also some super-tight fabrics that have some structure to them, such as the ones used for the iconic Hervé Léger bandage dresses. Those fabrics are chic and will enhance all curves.

Stretchy denim jeans should be quite thick so that they do not look like leggings (because leggings are in no way trousers). Other than that, they are always a good idea for curvy legs.

What to mix with bodycon

Something larger
As we know, fashion is all about balance. When rocking super-tight, rock-star leather trousers, you can totally afford to top them with an oversize knit that will take away some of their sexiness (and enable your colleagues to focus on their work).

The same goes if you opted for a skin-tight bodysuit: try matching it with an A-line or maxi skirt or some high-waisted, wide-legged trousers for a stylish contrast.

Something loose or fluid
But, hey, you don't *have* to go oversize. You could just as successfully choose a slightly loose T-shirt or shirt to tuck into those Mick Jaggerette leather trousers.

Something thicker
Or, wear super-tight yet super-thick high-waisted jeans with a skintight bodysuit.

A layer over the top
Voilà, you are wearing this super-tight dress/skirt/top, but you are not quite comfortable yet, or it is just cold, or you merely want to style it up. In all these cases, layering your bodycon dress with a long cardigan or a trench coat, or your bodycon top with a blazer or a fluffy cardigan, would be an excellent move.

The correct lingerie
You will definitely need to invest in some seamless underwear.

Fluidity & Softness

The shape of fluid clothes changes, depending on the body and the movement. Such pieces glide over the body and move around with you. Fluid fabrics should not have too much weight to them and should not cling to the body.

Fluid tops
• Make stiff clothes look more feminine.
• Look equally stylish worn tucked in or out.
• Disguise large breasts and your tummy.

Fluid bottoms
• Look amazing when they feature a lot of fabric, such as a long, flowy boho skirt.
• Are more forgiving in thicker fabrics that'll hold you better, such as a heavy satin that won't wrinkle and will glide over your legs.

Fluid dresses or jumpsuits
• Either go short and rather large or add a belt, otherwise you might appear shapeless.

What about jerseys and knits?
Jerseys and knits are never "fluid" as they "hug" the body rather than glide over it. Such soft clothes have no shape before you wear them and do not flow when you move. Typically, knits enter this "soft" category. The looser the knit, the softer the result.

Fluid fabrics shortlist

• Most silks
• Thin, non-jersey cottons
• Most polyesters
• Light, silk-like viscose
• Light lyocell

Must-have fluid tops:

• Button-up shirts
• Sleeveless tops
• Three-quarter-sleeve tops

Must-have soft clothes

- Loads of T-shirts
- Sweaters

How to wear soft clothes

• Tops
Soft tops will bring some casualness and femininity to more structured clothes. But loose-fit T-shirts are not as good as fluid tops at disguising a chubby top half.

• Dresses
Avoid shapeless T-shirt dresses or thin, loose sweater dresses. Instead, stick to those that look like actual oversize sweaters.

• Trousers
Unless you have an iron butt and legs, avoid soft trousers.

Long or Short?

Both very short and very long dresses can sound intimidating. But with a few simple tips you will soon be ready to embrace the extremes of the skirt world.

Mini skirts

Too obviously sexy, too young…But mini skirts or dresses are so much more than this: they can be elegant, boyish, flirty… If you fear showing your legs, wait for winter and the security blanket of opaque tights (pantyhose).

There is no rule against wearing the full sexy attire: a mini skirt, low-cut neckline, tight shape and high heels *can* be part of one single outfit. Even a classy one is achievable. But on a daily basis, you may want to play it more low-key (*see right*).

Very long skirts

Even though we may instantly imagine a princess gown whenever someone mentions a long length, there is more to this style than just the maxi skirt: you could also go for a super-long, tight dress or skirt (as long as it contains Lycra or a slit, you should be able to walk in it).

To keep your mini low-key:

- **Go for wider shapes**
  For instance, babydoll dresses, A-line skirts and oversize sweater dresses.

- **Cover the top half**
  With crew-neck tees, turtlenecks, oversize sweaters, blazers…

- **Top with longer layers**
  Trench coats, slouchy cardigans, tailored coats…

- **Wear flats**
  Since the mini skirt lengthens the leg, you can wear flat shoes without having a "short-leg" effect.

- **Be your casual self**
  Be rock, be androgynous, be sporty, be bohemian, be conservative, be fun…Most styles (other than sophisticated and sexy, of course) tend to remove the sexy feel of the mini skirt.

For long length that is more Parisian than princess:

- **Wear thick heels**
  Such as platforms or espadrilles, if your skirt/dress feels summery. Or try high-heeled boots peeking out from under the bottom of your skirt.

- **Layer something over the top**
  Going vertical will lighten your outfit, so add a coat, biker jacket, loose sweater, belted cardigan…

- **Add jewellery**
  Accessorizing will keep you away from the "all-fabric" look. Try a pair of oversize earrings and plenty of bracelets.

Farrah Ben Brahim

Age 26, salesperson and visual merchandizer

Farrah was kind enough to welcome me into her tiny little studio located just down the hill of Montmartre. Young Parisians often have to cope with small spaces and Farrah has definitely made the best use of the space she has. Pretty shelves with potted succulents, a tasteful display of coffee-table books and even an adorable kitten named Simba.

How would you describe your style?
That's complicated…I'd say minimalist and boyish. Yes, I definitely have a masculine side.

Did your style evolve?
It's funny you ask this question because I feel I want to evolve *now*. I have been working in retail and merchandising for years, but that is about to change. I want to try some more eccentric clothes, even though I'll stay true to myself: my style will remain minimalist.

Could you share some advice with us?
When you are shopping, don't think, "Oh, this dress is beautiful, I must buy it", but look for pieces that match your personality, body and all that you are. People with style are people who know themselves. Also, you should understand a garment and what it represents. For instance, you can wear a little flowery strappy dress with sneakers and a T-shirt underneath in a tomboy style, or you can play on its delicacy and wear it with bare shoulders and strappy sandals, for a more fragile attitude.

Do you follow trends?
I think trends make you daring. If you are not sure whether you would wear something, the coming trend gives you the courage to do so. Trends are created by people who dare and make others want to dare as well.

Do you dress for occasions?
I always dress pretty much the same. For a night out, I'll play with accessories: shoes, statement earrings and a great hairstyle.

What's your relationship with makeup?
I find it *emmerdant* ("boring and annoying"), to be honest. No need. And I don't see why we should be obligated to wear it when men aren't. Yes, if I want or have to, I'll use mascara, red lipstick and blush. And do my brows. Sometimes doing my brows can be my only makeup. But, as much as possible, I prefer to stay away from foundation – I don't like how it feels.

How would you describe Parisian style?
Refinement by simplicity. I've just come back from a month in the US, and girls want too much there. The bodycon dress, the long nails, the great hair…they show it all at the same time. French girls are more understated, I feel. But I do not like to make generalizations – Americans with great (even French girl-) style do exist.

Flats

How do we French fashion goddesses manage to stay so thin? We walk around the city all day and take the stairs in *le métro*. This is why we adore flats. But, hey, let's be honest, outfits always look best with a good pair of heels. So how to wear flats with flair? Let the ankle height of your flats determine what clothes you wear with them.

Flat boots

Such as…knee-high flat boots.

Why we love them
Because they are warm and dressy.

What to wear with them
My favourite option for a great silhouette is a knee-length skirt or dress, in order not to show any leg. Mini skirts or shorts that do show some leg *can* work, but should be saved for only the longest legs.

Beneath-the-ankle flats

Such as loafers, sneakers and derbies…

Why we love them
• They reveal the ankle and do not cut off the legs, making them look really long.
• Most of them have a boyish style.

What to wear with them
• Cropped trousers or any type of skirt.
• Wear with "invisible" socks in the summer, cute socks peeking out in the autumn and spring, and pull-on tights (pantyhose) in the winter.

"We walk around the city all day and take the stairs in le métro… This is why we adore flats"

Above-the-ankle flats

Such as low boots,
Dr Martens boots,
Converse high tops…

Why we love them
For their rebellious
style and protection
against Paris's lovely
(not) weather.

What to wear with them
• Cropped trousers
work well as they
reveal the top of the
shoes, as do short skirts,
dresses and shorts.
• These shoes tend to
accentuate the calves
and shorten the legs, so
they look better on girls
with slim calves and
long legs. To balance
the short-leg effect, opt
for short skirt lengths.

Low-vamp flats

Such as ballet flats,
pointy flats, some
sandals…

Why we love them
• Low-vamp shoes,
such as pointy or ballet
flats, elongate the leg
even more than shoes
with a high vamp.
• The downside is that
they also make long
feet look even longer.

What to wear with them
• Cropped trousers
are perfect for a fresh
Bardot-esque look.
• For skirts, any length
works, but pairing
ballet flats with a
midi-length skirt may
make you look older.
• Avoid pairing them
with long, skinny
trousers, or it will look
like you have forgotten
your shoes.

Heels

Everyone loves a heel. But one main tip from French girls to the rest of the world: higher is NOT better.

Before buying the shoe equivalent of a skyscraper, remember:
• You should always be able to walk in an elegant manner.
• Your feet should not look like hooves from the front.

When you aim to be comfortable, look for:
• Chunky heels for more stability.
• Some cushioning.
• An arch that isn't too steep (a platform helps to diminish this).

Some body related tips:
• The steeper the arch, the smaller the feet will look.
• The chunkier the heel, the slimmer the calves will look.

Here are some French girls' high-heel favourites and how to wear them…

Kitten heels

Kitten-heel shoes have low, small heels and no front platform.

What kitten heels?
When choosing your kitten heels, make sure:
• The shoe is not heavy-looking (if you want a closed toe, choose one that is slightly pointed).
• The heel is nicely balanced and does not sit too far toward the centre of the sole, nor protrude behind the heel.

What to wear with them
• Cropped trousers.

What not to wear with them:
• Wide, long trousers.
• Below-the-knee skirts may appear mumsy.

Ankle boots

Boots often have wide, low heels that will make you appear effortlessly leaner and taller.

What to wear with them
• They are the perfect match for a mini skirt or skinny jeans, no matter what your size.

What not to wear with them
• Below-the-knee skirts, because the height of the boots combined with the length of the skirt and low heels is likely to make your legs appear shorter.

Chunky high heels

They give gorgeous long legs and are comfy to wear on a daily basis. Knee-high boots can enter this category.

What to wear with them
- Cropped trousers
- Flared trousers
- Midi lengths
- Flowy skirts

What not to wear with them
- A short and bodycon dress, or anything that is too obviously sexy.

Wedges

Wedges have a chunky front platform and are therefore easy to walk in as long as they are not sky-high. Most wedges are sandals because as boots they would appear massive.

As you may not know, mini wedges exist and they might just be the most comfortable shoe ever created.

What to wear with them
- Everything, *mes chéries*
- Cropped trousers
- Below-the-knee skirts
- Short skirts
- Short shorts
- Flared trousers
- Tights (pantyhose), if the fabric of the shoes is not too summery.

Stiletto heels

Stilettos are shoes with very thin heels; in French we also call them "*talons aiguilles*", which literally translates as "needle heels". They are very sexy and made household names of shoe designers such as Christian Louboutin and Manolo Blahnik.

Stilettos start at 7.5cm (3in) high and can reach 15.5cm (6in). I think the best height is 10 or 13cm (4 or 5in) because it does not require a platform. For me and, as far as I have seen on the street, for most *Parisiennes*, the stiletto heel does not involve a heavy platform on the front. These heels can be attached to boots as well as court shoes.

What to wear with them
- Cropped trousers
- Midi lengths

Les Attaches

Or an explanation of the French woman's paradox: how the hell can they be super-sexy when they play it the opposite of sexy?

For instance, imagine a woman. She is wearing minimal makeup, bed hair, an oversize sweater, jeans…This doesn't sound like a really attractive outfit, does it?

But wait until you've played the French magic trick. Crop the jeans, roll up the sleeves of the oversize sweater, throw on some sexy heels and, boom, you've achieved that effortless French-girl style.

This outfit is more revealing than you would think because it directs the focus to "*les attaches*", which would translate as "the joints". We consider them as sexy a body part to highlight as any other.

(A word of caution: only draw attention to these areas if they are part of your assets.)

How to draw attention to *les attaches*:

- Roll up your sleeves and your trousers.

- Invest in three-quarter and cropped lengths for both arms and legs.

- DIY cuts – mostly to transform full-length trousers into cropped ones.

- Wear jewellery – both a most delicate wrist chain or a chunky bracelet will embellish your elegant wrists.

- Wear tights (pantyhose), or socks, or anything that will draw attention to your ankles when the weather is too cold for bare skin.

To Belt or Not to Belt?

Since most trousers and skirts are fitted to our frame, wearing a belt is often more a style choice than a necessity. The easiest and most usual way to wear a belt is at the waistband of trousers or a skirt but you can also use it to cinch an outfit.

"Since your choice of belting spot will define the shape of your body, choose it according to your body shape"

Where to belt

Besides sometimes being a good way to accessorize an outfit, a belt is useful for adding some shape to it. Therefore the outfit has to have some fabric to shape up (belting a completely bodycon outfit that doesn't include trousers looks odd).

Since your choice of belting spot will define the shape of your body, I strongly advise you to choose it according to your body shape.

High belting

If you have a defined waist, accentuating it with a belt is a clever style move. You can achieve this by adding a belt or by choosing an outfit with a built-in belt (wrap dresses are your best friends).

But if you have a thick waist, I recommend you stay away from this style: trying to create the illusion of a defined waist with a belt doesn't work and, worse, it will only draw attention to the fact that your waist is not so well defined.

Be sure to place your belt where your waist is tiniest. Belting below or slightly above this will make your waist appear much bigger than it actually is.

Sometimes I hear my clients worrying that the belt will create a "round tummy underneath"; it may, but only you will notice it. All other eyes will be on your wonderful hourglass figure.

High belting is also a great way to create the illusion of longer legs.

Empire belting

This is a handy trick when you want to give your figure some structure but you have a round tummy.

Place the belt on your ribcage, just under your boobs (but make sure they do not hide the belt).

Low-slung belt

A good option for giving structure to your figure if you don't have a defined waist.

Women who have a defined waist can also adopt this style, but those who have significantly large hips should avoid it.

If you are short-waisted, wearing a low-slung belt is a clever way to elongate your torso.

Feminine & Androgynous

You will look "feminine", no matter what you are wearing: a woman is, by definition, feminine. That said, some clothing shapes are classically linked to femininity – basically, those that rely on feminine assets or supposed feminine character traits. Clothes that relate to men's classic work outfits or to sports are considered "androgynous" or "masculine" (you know, because in the past women didn't take part in those activities).

You can wear all feminine or all androgynous, or a mix of different styles to reflect your personality and give a new dimension to your look. Take a high-waisted, flouncy red mini skirt, for example. You could wear it with:
• A fluid burgundy camisole and espadrille wedges (for an ultra-feminine look)
• A black-and-white striped polo shirt and black skater sneakers
• A loose-fitting, washed-out, black AC/DC tee with pointy, high-heel, black ankle boots
• A fluffy, pink short-sleeved knit with black patent loafers
• A white shirt and a black blazer with flat, black Chelsea boots

A dark grey suit with a buttoned white shirt and classic black derbies is totally an option if the cuts are perfect (when it comes to "menswear", tailoring is everything). You could even add a "dandy touch" with some coloured or glittery socks (hey, we aren't men, all right?), patent leather or gold derbies, or an unusual print on the shirt.

Classic feminine touches

• Outline your waistline
• Wear heels
• Expose your back
• Wear flowy fabrics
• Wear flounces or ruffles
• Reveal your shoulders
• Show cleavage

Androgynous options

• Suits
• Stiff cotton button-up shirts
• *Richelieus*/Oxfords
• Derbies
• Loafers
• Ties and bowties
• Blazers
• Chinos
• Carrot trousers
• Cigarette trousers

Try them with:

• Long, wavy hair
• Bold red lips
• Red nails
• Stiletto heels
• Graphic eyeliner
• A suit in a pink fabric

Chapter 4

Wardrobe Essentials

The Parisian Approach to Wardrobe Essentials

Essentials may differ from one wardrobe to the next. But what they do have in common is that they are super-versatile and timeless. Versatile because you can match an essential with pretty much anything. Timeless because a good essential, or basic, shouldn't age, at least not very quickly (a good hint is if you can't remember the year you bought it).

Owning a good range of basics enables you to put together endless combinations with your most daring garments and accessories. No basics = morning struggle to get dressed = busy look = grumpy mood. Yes, basics even improve your mental health, so invest time (and money) in finding your perfect essentials. Afterall, they are going to be your regular partners for the coming years.

Main rule: a good basic should be minimal – no red stitching on your jeans; no glitzy shoulders on your grey cashmere. That said, your essentials are yours to define and the combinations of them is very personal.

You don't have to own "all the essentials" but you should have one of them in each category. A timeless coat, a timeless top, a timeless pair of heels and flats…you get the idea. But what kind of timelessness it is is your call. Don't like the trench coat? Get a tailored black coat or a jean jacket instead…Just choose whatever seems to fit your personality.

In this chapter I review the most common French wardrobe staples and give tips on how to wear them. Pick yours.

"Essentials are yours to define…Just choose whatever seems to fit your personality"

The Trench Coat

Trenches have a classic, timeless feel that
I love. They also have the magic power to
soften any look that seems too daring, giving
it a hint of typically French conservative
nonchalance. Whatever your style is, you
can trench it up (which sounds rather like
an advertising slogan).

How to choose it

The classic trench coat is made from quite stiff fabric and has buttons on the shoulders and down the front, plus a vent at the back. That said, some contemporary versions are more fluid and others lack buttons…

Choose a trench that suits your personal style – is it classic or minimalist? – and your figure.

- If you are petite, choose a short trench (mid-thigh length).
- If you are tall, choose a long, fluid trench.
- If you have a round belly and no defined waist, choose an unbelted trench without a structured waist (a belted trench will do you no favours).

In terms of colour, you should start with THE beige trench, before considering other shades. I suggest you avoid black and navy blue in the stiff versions, as somehow they appear too strict, while bold colours can feel overwhelming. Instead, look for the in-betweens: pastels, fun prints…

You could also own various shapes of beige trench, such as a short stiff one and a long fluid one.

How to style it

Heels are a must to contrast with the trench's classic, almost boyish, vibe. They'll also be especially useful in lengthening the silhouette if you are shorter than 1.7m (5ft 7in) in height.

If you are quite petite but not in a heel mood, go for a short trench, wear flatforms or just wear your trench unbuttoned.

Actually, unless it's pouring with rain, wear your trench open, with the belt casually knotted at the back. If you need to close it, knot the belt at one side (and don't use the built-in buckle).

There's no need to wear something underneath, either. Carine Roitfeld, former editor-in-chief of French *Vogue*, said that Parisian style is wearing a trench with nothing underneath.

What to wear with it

1. A basic style
I know basic + basic can sound super-dull… But what if those basics are cut to perfection and tastefully accessorized? Yes to a trench coat with mom jeans, a white T-shirt and a pair of chunky high heels.

2. A girly style
You know that little summery dress with flounces, which makes you feel like you are five? Trench it up to make it look grown-up and effortless.

3. A sexy style
That black mini dress and stiletto heels are perfect for your date but too much for *le métro*? Trench them up.

4. A casual or rock style
Aiming to make your washed-out jeans and worn-out sneakers look chic? Add a trench.

The Cool Factor Jacket

Layers are always a cool way to upgrade the style stakes of an outfit. And cool layers are even better. I especially like stylish jackets that you can wear either as an outer layer or under a coat. You can use them as a mid-season cover-up, for warm layering in the winter or to look cool in a club.

Top three

1. The biker jacket

A leather biker jacket will give any outfit a rock edge. Choose short (waist length) or oversize (hip length). A short biker jacket will look more refined than an oversize one.

Wear a short biker jacket over longer layers – T-shirts, slouchy sweaters, classy tops or oversize dresses – to add structure.

Wear tight, bodycon or short clothes under your oversize biker jacket to avoid a bulky look.

2. The jean jacket

If you want to look like a cool kid, remember that your jean jacket should not look brand new. You have two options: either search for an old one in a thrift store, or get a new one that looks like it's old.

This jacket should not:
• Have any stretch fabric in it (or at least look like it doesn't).
• Be cinched.
• Have any obvious fake wear marks.

It could be short (waist length) or oversize (hip length). The short version should fit close to the body. The oversize one should have a fuller back – bomber-jacket style.

You could have fun and customize one with dye, embroidery, drawing pens…there are endless options.

Wear over T-shirts, dressy tops, sweaters, dresses…pretty much anything you like.

3. The bomber jacket

A fun piece for your wardrobe, the bomber jacket is not very versatile as it often comes in various colours, fabrics and shapes. (Although there are also basic bomber jackets in neutral shades that can be matched just like the jean jacket).

Mix your busy, "statement" bomber with basics, such as jeans, plain T-shirts and straight dresses.

Just like the other two styles, you can choose a short or long version.

The Tailored Coat

Winter is always too long. One of the reasons being that you always have to wear the same coats over and over again, because you probably do not have that many. Maybe you even own only one…because:

• Coats are expensive.

• You are a Parisian (or a Londoner, or a New Yorker…) and, the property market being what it is, your wardrobe is not extensive: coats take up space.

• Finding a coat is such a pain that you procrastinate until your only coat dies of old age.

Since you are going to wear your coat for four or more winters in a row, until it falls to bits, you had better choose it wisely. Which is why I suggest you go for a tailored coat because it will always make you look elegant.

The most important thing is that your coat has structure. Then the shape doesn't matter. It can have straight, masculine lines, a cinched waist, be rather short or very long…In the end, it should be a coat that will make you look chic and stylish every day.

If you find your coat and it's true love, you can be wedded to it till death do you part (three to five years later, according to its average coat–life expectancy).

Style tip

If you own only one coat, go for a neutral colour that will be the most versatile, in a style you won't get tired of. You should be able to accessorize it in various ways.

Dresses

The good thing about dresses is that you do not need to create an outfit. You just need the right shoes to pair it with, maybe some cute accessories and, boom, you're good to go.

In the spirit of laziness (that we call effortlessness or nonchalance) and for when you have limited thinking time in the morning, build yourself a small collection of summer dresses and jumpsuits. They are perfect for warmer days when it is too hot to wear anything else (one of those moments when you really are thankful to be a woman) and if it gets a bit colder, just throw on a layer: a loose cardigan, a trench coat, a blazer, a biker jacket, a jean jacket…

It is also handy to own a bunch of dressy dresses (or dressy jumpsuits, for that matter) in case of unexpected social events.

Top dressy dresses

1. Little black dress (LBD)
It should fit you to perfection and be simple, without too much detailing, so that you can dress it down or up from day to night. With such a neutral canvas, you can have fun with daring accessories.

2. Brightly coloured cocktail dress
Because there will always be a wedding to attend, right? The colour should enhance your complexion and the shape flatter your body. Chances are you'll wear it more than once so make sure you love it… unless you decide to rent one (clever).

3. Evening dress
For when you need something more couture than your LBD. Maybe a jumpsuit. Maybe some sequins or lamé. Or transparency. Or an unexpected cut. (The renting trick is an even cleverer move with this one).

4. Chic warm dress
Layering dresses can be super-annoying, so you should own one dressy wintertime dress to wear to events at that time of year.

Top summer dresses

1. Office dress

Smart enough and discreetly stylish, the work dress saves you when the air conditioning is broken. Wear it with elegant sandals (and an impecable pedicure), court shoes or ballet flats.

2. City dress

Find one that suits your style and feels dressy enough for the city cobblestones. Then match it with open flats or platform sandals.

3. Beach dress

Flowy or mini is what you are looking for (to get some air). For a holiday, always pack one or two easy-to-wear dresses, open flats and platform sandals, plus some not-too-precious jewellery.

Jeans

I have overheard older American women saying that French women don't wear jeans. Today, you just have to walk five minutes along a denim-filled Parisian street to realize that nothing is less accurate. I even think *les Parisiennes* perhaps wear jeans more than any other women in the world. *La Parisienne* likes to follow denim trends, so she'll buy the new style and also keep her old pair.

The colours

The four classic jeans colours are:
1. dark blue (also called raw jeans)
2. light blue (from medium to whitened)
3. white
4. black (from super-dark to washed-out)

I do not recommend grey jeans, which almost always make outfits look dull.

Since there is no need to own 16 pairs of jeans (even if they all are different), I suggest you own each shape (*see* pages 108–9) in a different colour.

Always avoid jeans that look like they have been artificially aged and instead buy an undistressed pair that'll wash out over the years.

"Les Parisiennes perhaps wear jeans more than any other women in the world"

Shapes

Skinny jeans

These jeans contain elastane to hug your curves. Yet they should not contain TOO MUCH elastane or they will end up looking like denim-print leggings instead of actual jeans. They may be either high-waisted or low-waisted, full-length or cropped.

How to style them

Shape-wise, it is like wearing bare legs, which is perfect to balance oversize outfits on the upper part of your body. You can wear the full-length ones with low boots and the cropped version with pumps, sandals or ballet flats. I do not recommend wearing long skinnies with ballet flats, though, as this creates a long-foot effect.

Are they for me?

Contrary to what you may think at first glance, skinnies flatter every girl with curves, whether she is skinny or voluptuous. They look wonderful on muscular, well-shaped legs and they make hips appear smaller by not adding any width to them. If your legs lack curves, however, opt for one of the other shapes of jeans.

Slim jeans

Slim jeans follow the curves but are not bodycon.

How to style them

Just like skinny jeans (*see left*).

Are they for me?

Choose them rather than skinnies if you fear cellulite showing or don't want to emphasize your calves.

Flared jeans

These should be tight on the hips and flare out from either below the hips (classic flared jeans) or below the knees (often called bell-bottom jeans). Classic flared jeans look better high-waisted, while bell-bottom jeans can be high- or low-waisted.

How to style them

Their width tends to shorten the silhouette, so wear with platform shoes and let your jeans hang over them for long-looking legs.

In 2015 a trend for "cropped flares" emerged. These look best if you are of average height. Pair with mid-height boots, ankle boots or heels.

Are they for me?

Perfect for anyone with broad hips and/or chunky thighs as the flare will balance them. This style is also great for adding "body" to stick-thin legs.

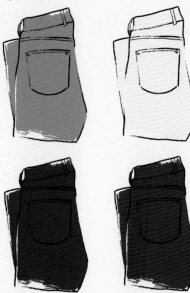

Boyfriend jeans

These are oversized jeans with a dropped waist. They should be worn low on the hips with the pockets low on the butt. Boyfriend jeans are low-waisted; if they are not, either they are girlfriend jeans or you are wearing them wrong.

How to style them

The droopy, saggy shape may be stylish and cool but, let's face it, this is clearly not the most flattering. Roll them up to reveal sexy ankles and wear with under-the-ankle flats, kitten or high heels.

Are they for me?

They look fab on androgynous women, tall and skinny women, and curvy, sporty ladies with round butts and muscular legs. Avoid these jeans if you've skipped the gym for some time and own a jelly-like bottom.

Mom jeans

Typically, these are the 501 Levi jeans, featuring a narrow, high waist and straight legs. You could wear them cropped or rolled up. If the legs feel too wide, you could have them slimmed down by a tailor.

How to style them

These jeans are meant to reveal your waistline so tuck your tops in or choose cropped tops. Since the legs are quite wide, I suggest you always let some ankle show. Low flats, pumps and ankle boots look good with them.

Are they for me?

If you own a defined waistline, yes!

Details

Pockets

Tinier pockets create rounder and more voluminous-looking butts. High pockets give the illusion of high butts, whereas dropped pockets make butts look flat.

Hem

Jeans almost always need to be shortened. I speak from experience; only the tallest girls do not need any altering done to their jeans. Get the alteration done immediately after purchase. It is totally forbidden (by the fashion police) to walk around with a *faux* hem – those inside folds are fooling no one. Even if you intend to roll the hem up for style, you still need to have it shortened, otherwise you'll end up with a super-thick, inelegant roll at the bottom.

When in doubt about the length of your jeans, cut them to the bottom of your heel. You'll still be able to roll them up if you want to. For flared jeans, remember that you'll always wear them with heels (unless you are super-tall with long legs and so can afford to wear flats).

Always ask your tailor to restitch the sewing line on the hem. IN THE SAME COLOUR.

Stitching

A lightly contrasting stitching is best: it gives definition while remaining discreet.

Styling

Once, you have the basics nailed, you could try experimenting with some eccentric colours, funky patchwork or embroidery…

Shirts

What could be more of a timeless basic than a shirt? It can be either casual or sophisticated, or even both simultaneously. Thanks to its buttons and details it always looks interesting. There is no need to do a lot to make it stylish: some button opening, some sleeve rolling *et voilà*. (Well, also some ironing. I know, this is about the worst… Hire a pick-up dry cleaner.)

How to choose it

Timeless shirt checklist
- Quality buttons: either pretty (mother-of-pearl, bone…) or discreet.
- Invisible stitching: you should not see the stitching especially around the buttonholes).
- Quality fabric: the fabric should not shine (unless it is intentional).
- Good fit: your shirt should not create a horizontal fold when you wear it (otherwise it is too tight).
- Perfect collar: a classic collar should look right both open and closed. Some refined collars, such as a Peter Pan or Victorian collar, can only be worn closed.

The fabric
It can be either loose or have some stiffness to it but it should never be bodycon. In other words, it can contain stretch for comfort but should NOT actually be stretched.

How to wear it

Fully tucked in

Great with high-waisted bottoms. If your shirt is loose-fitting, make it slightly full and blousy. If it is tight, make sure it is not creating unflattering folds.

If wearing with low-waisted bottoms, ensure your shirt is extra long, so that it doesn't escape every time you sit down. Not the best if you wish to hide a chubby tummy.

To tuck your shirt neatly into your skirt, lift up your skirt and pull your shirt down from the inside. Give the shirt a little fullness above the waistline if needed.

Tucking your shirt in is a good trick if you have big boobs and a flat tummy because it will make the "tent" effect created by your breasts disappear.

Untucked

Perfect with low-waisted bottoms or high-waisted bodycon bottoms.

If you have a belly to cover, or are aiming to make wide hips look narrower, go for this style. If you are very tiny, this style will give you a little more fullness and volume.

Half-tucked

Achieved by tucking only the front of your shirt into low-waisted bottoms. Tuck in either one side or both sides of the shirt. Let the rest hang out from the sides of your hips to cover your rear for a cool and sexy style.

Perfect for revealing a flat tummy and/or curvy hips.

(Maybe one day we'll see a reverse half-tucking in order to show your bum and hide your stomach? But let's not get ahead of ourselves.)

Knotted

If your shirt is too long, undo one or two buttons at the bottom and casually knot the ends in the front.

This is a good trick to look summery and show off your curves.

Rolled-up sleeves

With their long sleeves and buttoned collar, shirts sometimes look too strict. Lighten them up by displaying more skin. Rolling up your sleeves will also give a casual, effortless style.

For a rolled sleeve that looks neat and will stay put all day long: fold your sleeve up to where you want it to be (around 5cm/2in below the elbow), then double fold. Once you have achieved this expert roll, add some bracelets to complete your outfit.

Open collar

Another way to make a shirt look sexier is to unbutton it down to the cleavage point (where you see "in between" the boobs).

If you do not have a visible cleavage point, you can dare to wear it *à la* Jane Birkin for the night-time, with your shirt open to just above your bellybutton. It's a rather daring way to display *des bijoux de beau* ("beautiful delicate jewellery").

An open collar works when you have broad shoulders because it adds a visual break to the width of your *carrure* ("shoulders").

Buttoned collar

This "good student" style can be a fun way to blow hot and cold. Wear it with a mini skirt, mini shorts or just classic trousers. It is all about the attitude: there is no need to always show skin.

T-shirts

T-shirts have definitely become Parisian wardrobe staples. As their name indicates, they are shaped like the letter T, and as their name does not indicate, they are made from jersey knit. They are the blank canvases you can layer anything on: funky jackets, kimonos, statement jewellery, huge belts… If you are a T-shirt kind of lady, you should get yourself a small collection of them.

How to choose it

Colour

One white, one grey and one black will always come in handy. Generally, coloured T-shirts need to be dressed up, whereas neutral T-shirts will look effortlessly stylish (but, hey, accessorizing is always key with basics). Bold shades can look too sporty, and pastel shades can resemble nightgowns.

Print

Graphic prints look fun. It could be a band T-shirt, a vintage touristy one – or anything cool. Hunt them out in thrift stores.

All-over prints (except stripes) are trickier: on jersey T-shirts they may look like pyjamas.

Detailing

An embellished T-shirt is rarely a good idea: it won't be enough to turn the T-shirt into a statement piece, yet it will be annoying enough to make the T-shirt difficult to match. I am talking mini studs, tiny embroidery, sparkly patches… Instead, use jewellery and accessories to decorate your T-shirt.

Fabric

Cotton and linen are perfect and the fluidity of viscose is interesting. You can find T-shirts in funky fabrics, but they aren't a blank canvas.

Shape

V-necks and scoop necks look sexier and are easy to layer. Go for low necklines if you can. Crew necks look sportier and are trickier to layer as the high neckline can show.

Avoid long-sleeved T-shirts, which look like sad pyjamas, unless you are layering them under other pieces.

Always check that the seams are flat.

Style tip

Let the bottom of your
T-shirt show beneath
your sweater: it will
create a layer of
a different colour
between your top
and your bottoms,
just like a belt would.

Dressy Tops

Sometimes you just want to be slightly dressy: not over the top, just effortlessly chic. Which is when you need a dressy top in your wardrobe. It could be made of a precious fabric (silk, silky polyester) or have a sophisticated cut (ruffles, cut-outs, a low V-neck), beautiful embellishments (embroidery, a graphic print, ornaments), a stunning colour, a wonderful print… Or all of the above at the same time.

How to style it

Bottoms

If your top is elaborate, keep your bottoms basic. If your top is dressy, yet has a simple shape and a neutral colour, you could pair it with something more eccentric. For example, you can choose to wear your top with:
- Something equally sophisticated, such as cigarette trousers, a mini skirt or a pencil skirt, if you are going to a dressy event.
- Casual jeans, to create a contrast, if you are going to a semi-casual event.

Shoes

You could match your dressy top with chic shoes or worn-out sneakers as a contrast.

Jewellery

If your dressy top has a simple shape and is a plain colour, you could complement it with either a statement necklace or some statement earrings.

If it has a more elaborate shape, you could skip jewellery altogether or just go for statement earrings.

"If your top is elaborate, keep your bottoms basic"

The Timeless Sweater

In other words: a sweater you can wear with everything. To qualify as timeless, it should be a neutral colour, a simple cut and a discreet knit, so it matches each and every one of your wintertime bottoms.

How to choose it

I recommend owning one winter cashmere because it is warm, smooth and not bulky.

If you own only one, I suggest you choose grey, the perfect match-everything colour. (Bonus: it doesn't show pale or dark dust…) Black, navy blue and beige are also excellent neutrals.

The sweater's shape should be slightly loose. Get it with a V-neck, a crew neck or a turtleneck, depending on which best suits your body and your style.

How to style it

In winter, replace your shirts and T-shirts with sweaters. Better still, wear your sweaters on top of them so that you have an interesting base layer on show. For work, your sweater will be the ideal companion to dress down your pencil skirt, your cigarette trousers or your blazer.

Must-have sweaters

- Different colours of a basic shape.
- An oversize sweater with a chunky knit.
- Dressy sweaters (with ruffles, sequins, a special knit…) that do not need to be accessorized.
- Different necklines that suit you.
- A bodycon sweater to wear with high-waisted bottoms.

Style tips

- Layer your dress with a sweater instead of a cardigan, transforming it into a skirt.
- Roll up the sleeves of your sweater to make it look casual and cool.

The Blazer

Aaaah, *la Parisienne* and her blazer: a true
love story. More elegant than any other layer,
but not as formal as you might think. You
can wear it for a dressy occasion as well as
for a casual day in the city.

How to choose it?

The fit
The shoulder seams
of the blazer should
exactly follow the line
of your own shoulders.
You need to be able
to move around in
your blazer (but this
doesn't mean doing
your morning yoga
routine in it, OK?). If it
is comfortable enough
to type on your laptop
without experiencing
any stretching on the
upper arms, go for
it. And you should be
able to fasten the front
button…even if you
intend to wear it open.

The shape

For an elegant yet relaxed style, opt for structured shoulders (without obvious added padding) along with a soft material.

The hip-length, single-breasted, one-button blazer (with optional super-slight cinching) will suit most body shapes and give your silhouette that effortless chic look you have been searching for.

If you have a tiny waist and rounded hips, you may prefer a belted or cinched blazer to outline your curves.

A shorter blazer can be interesting for cool layering options.

The bigger the collar, the more masculine the look. Have you tried a collarless blazer?

The fabric

Wool is perfect for structured blazers while high-quality polyesters are very good for fluidity.

Linen is a light and elegant option for the summertime – if you don't mind the creases.

Canvas blazers keep their shape, while jersey blazers lose theirs quite quickly.

The colour

As a blazer is a wardrobe staple, again I recommend you first go for neutrals. Black and navy blue are year-round favourites while white and nude are very useful to wear with summer outfits.

How to wear it

An open blazer will almost always be your best choice: it shows your top and jewellery underneath while creating vertical lines that slim the silhouette. However, to accentuate your waistline, button it up.

How to style it

Jeans

A blazer slung on over a casual outfit is an iconic Parisian mix. Wear it with jeans, on top of casual T-shirts or dressy tops.

A mini skirt/dress

Mixing sexy and androgynous is also a Parisian trademark.

Cigarette trousers

Of course, this is the style of trousers with which the blazer was designed to be worn. Why not dress them down with a T-shirt or a sweater instead of a shirt? For the evening, you could even wear the blazer topless and braless (*mon Dieu!*).

The Cardigan

I agree with some of you here, "cardigan" does not sound like the most exciting piece of clothing in the wardrobe. But it is a fashionable way to be warm and remain stylish as it covers the shoulders, back and arms while revealing the layers underneath.

How to choose it

Just like sweaters (*see* page 116), cardigans come in all kinds of fabrics, from fluffy angora knits to super-thin cashmere and silk blends. Choose them according to the weather and what you are wearing underneath (a thin fabric may wrinkle if the base layer is too stiff or too bulky).

Thin cardigans are perfect if you are looking for a slimming effect as they create vertical lines that elongate the body. For most people the perfect length is mid-hip or just below the bottom. Shorter may make you look square if the cardigan is large; longer works only if you are tall.

You can go for an understated style and just use the cardigan as a warm layer or opt for a more eccentric colour and style to make it the statement piece of your outfit.

How to wear it

Short cardigan
Almost always made of a thin fabric, this type of cardigan looks very well behaved. It suits women with a tiny torso (the fabric will stretch on girls with a curvy chest or arms).

I like to wear this style of cardigan buttoned with nothing underneath, as if it were a sweater, but you can wear them unbuttoned as a top layer (just make sure it doesn't look bulky).

Mid-to-long cardigan
From hip-length to mid-thigh length and from thin to very chunky.

The best way to wear it is open, as a warm layer over your other clothes. Many do not have buttons but if yours does and it's a loose fit, do up just one or two of them. This style looks good with tight-fitting bottoms to balance the silhouette.

Have fun with the base
The main advantage of the cardigan is that it shows the layer underneath while half-hiding it. If you have chosen a basic-looking cardigan, play with base layers in funky prints and unusual colours and add some accessories.

The Work Basics

Maybe you belong to that constantly shrinking part of the population who has to dress in a formal manner for the office (look on the bright side, this also means less trouble trying to look trendy every day)? Or maybe you have a rather free work dress code but still aim to look professional?

In either of these situations, it is always handy to own a few "office-proof" pieces that will make you look professional whether mixed with either other conventional pieces or more casual ones.

Nine office-proof wardrobe staples

1. A blazer
Wear it as part of a suit or with a classic shirt, if you have to be conservative, or dare to be more trendy with a T-shirt and clean sneakers, if you can.

2. Tailored trousers
You know, those classic straight wool trousers that could be half of a suit? They could be pressed with a front crease or not, with or without pockets, skinny or flared…If they are pressed, always make sure that the crease is not stretched by your thighs and check that the side pockets do not stick out or gape open (they tend to be more mischievous than jeans' pockets).

You could wear them with a classic blazer or give them a modern twist and pair them with casual clothes. If they are cropped, make them eccentric with funky socks or metallic shoes.

3. A pencil skirt
This is the feminine equivalent to tailored trousers, so you do not need to own both. (But, hey, it is always fun to have an alternative.)

The hem of your skirt can sit anywhere from just above the knees to just below, and it can have a slit or not. You'll feel more comfortable if it contains some stretch (you know, for walking).

4. A button-up shirt in a neutral shade or with stripes
You can wear it with other "office" pieces or break it up with jeans or a mini skirt (in a jeans-and-mini-skirt-friendly office).

5. Court shoes
Nothing says "working woman" more than killer heels. To ensure your look remains professional remember that the higher the heels, the longer the skirt. Or wear trousers.

6. Loafers or derbies
Dress like your male counterparts with masculine preppy shoes (*and* get equal pay?). I love them with cropped trousers, pencil skirts or a short skirt or dress.

7. A timeless bag that can fit your laptop
A plain, sturdy leather bag in a neutral colour with a classic design.

8. An office dress
One that just needs shoes to be complete. What could be better than an effortless start to your working day?

9. A tie
Just kidding. Even men have stopped wearing them. But, hey, as a statement piece in an eccentric look?

"What could be better than an effortless start to your working day?"

The Classy Flats

All women should own classy flats. Because our feet need a rest. Because we need to run for *le métro* (even though the next one will come in four minutes: an eternity to a Parisian). Because we may have pocket-sized boyfriends (like the former First Lady Carla Bruni). Because some of us walk like newborn giraffes when we're wearing heels…For all these reasons, it is useful to own at least two pairs of classy flats: one for winter, one for summer.

Classy winter flats

1. Loafers

These androgynous shoes have a Michael Jackson vibe and, as such, should always be impeccable. Polish as often as possible.

Since the shape itself is timeless, you could dare to go for a funky colour, a fun fabric or both. They'll look rad with cropped trousers/shorts/skirts/dresses.

2. Derbies/Richelieus/Oxfords

Choose those with noticeable soles and a toe that is neither too round nor too pointy: super-thin soles and rounded toes give the illusion of baby feet and thick calves; pointy toes make feet look longer than they actually are.

More traditional and masculine than loafers, they are often available in classic shades. You can make them look more fun by wearing them with funky socks or tights (pantyhose).

3. Creepers

Go for these very thick-soled lace-up shoes if you want to add a touch of eccentricity to your style. They are also perfect for keeping your feet dry in the Parisian rain.

The thick soles will elongate short legs and make calves look more slender.

Classy summer flats

You know that moment in the summer when you have to go to work, but your feet do not agree to slip into any pair of shoes other than flip-flops? Yet we all have to admit, they do not look very professional. That's why you absolutely need to own one pair of elegant "breezy" flats. (Another reason we have the dressing advantage over our male counterparts.)

1. Ballet flats

Adorable if you have delicate ankles, these also look youthful worn with cropped trousers, flowy skirts and jeans. Downside: they may make your feet sweaty in less than three seconds and are not the best choice if you have thick ankles and calves. Avoid matching them with stiff, below-the-knee skirts and dresses: the end result can be really mumsy.

Choose those with a thin sole, without any heavy ornament: ballet flats should feel light.

2. Open flats

Basically, these are ballet flats that let your feet breathe, without showing too much foot so they remain classy. Style them just like ballet flats. The opening can be in different places (peeptoes, slingbacks, side openings…).

3. Pointy flats

A pointy toe instantly makes a pair of flats look dressier. But forget about them if you have long feet as they will elongate them even more. Style them just like the former two flats.

Summer Sandals

In the middle of summer, you need a light version of everything in your wardrobe, including a flat and a heeled pair of sandals. But before you even think of shopping for sandals, you need a pedicure. I hate to be dictatorial about what women should do but…that's the price you pay for being allowed to show your feet. Actually, men wearing sandals should get pedis, too (say *non* to dirty toenails and cracked heels).

When buying sandals, be extra cautious:
• No glue should be showing.
• Under-sole stitching is best on flats.
• No toe should be escaping from the sides.
• No swelling should be experienced (your feet aren't French *saucissons*).
• Your feet should be contained WITHIN the shoe; the fact that it is "open-air" isn't an excuse to buy a pair that is too small.

What colour?
As usual, if you opt for only one pair of each, go for the neutrals. You can have more fun with the next pair. Nude and camel leather are definitely summer staples; they make the foot look as if it were naked. Gold also has this pretty "nude foot" effect. As does silver, if your skin has some snow-white undertones. Black can be very graphic and super-elegant.

What material?
Natural materials, such as leather, cotton or rope, are always excellent choices because they let the feet breathe and they age quite well. On the other hand, synthetics may make your feet sweat (and slip).

The essential sandals

1. Flat sandals

A thick sole will save you from backache, burning asphalt, rain and street dust, while a thin sole is definitely gorgeous on delicate feet but very fragile (so have it re-soled before it breaks).

2. Heeled sandals

Dressier than platforms, these can go from square kitten heels to stilettos. As seen in Sexy Heels (see pages 128–9), smaller heels are the most suitable for daytime styles, whether on holiday or at a toe-friendly office. Chunky-heeled sandals are an option for adding height while remaining comfortable to walk in (perfect for weddings). Stilettos are dream shoes when you can afford taxis and won't be confronted by soft grass or irregular pavements (red-carpet anyone?).

When purchasing heeled sandals, ensure that the material isn't too slippery or sweat-inducing and that you aren't sliding forward. An ankle strap can hold your feet in place (but is only flattering for women with slim ankles). If you really need it, you could invest in anti-slide insoles. Ultimately, your toes should not be clinging to the edge of your shoes like an owl perching on a branch.

If you have purchased your heeled sandals in April and can't wait, enjoy wearing them with socks or tights (pantyhose). These can be elegant or fun, with glitter, print or colour.

3. Platforms

My favourite summer shoes. Just as comfy as flats, if not more so. You can find platforms with a very low wedge that almost feel like you are not wearing heels. Or even opt for the Japanese-looking "flatforms", which are very conceptual but create giant feet – you have been warned.

Platforms are perfect if you have muscular or curvy legs, since their chunkiness makes your legs appear thinner. If you have super-tiny calves, avoid the chunkiest and highest versions.

Check that the shoes are steady – there is no shortage of uneven pavements in Paris.

Style tip

Flat summer sandals do not really enjoy being worn with socks as it'll make their owners resemble monks.

Sexy Heels

To be irresistible you don't need much more than a pair of sexy heels. The day you feel you look like a pumpkin in boyfriend jeans and an oversize knit, your sexy heels will magically transform you into Cinderella. Imagine their power when worn with a little black dress!

But can heels be sexy per se? In the end, isn't it the girl inside the heel who qualifies as such? *Oui et non.* There are some fetishists who like the shoe for itself (I know some of you who buy heels simply for the sole pleasure of owning them).

How to choose them?

Some defining features of sexy heels:

- A steep arch
- At least a 9cm (3½in) heel
- Not too much front platform (we can discuss later whether you find it sexy or not)
- A delicate design

The heels themselves can be either stiletto or square. The shoe could be courts, peeptoes, ankle boots, or knee- or thigh-high boots.

Last but not least, you should be able to walk elegantly in them. If they hurt, it shouldn't show, because there is nothing less appealing than someone who is insecure in her shoes. If dressy flats are what you are most comfortable walking in, they should be your sexy shoes and you can skip the skyscraper heels.

Top three sexy heels

1. Sexy courts/pumps

We all know the power of nonchalantly wearing clothes stolen from your boyfriend (or brother). We all know the power of sexy heels. So why not wear them together? Try with anything oversize: a blazer, all sorts of trousers and so on.

Use as a confidence-boosting weapon at work by teaming them with pencil skirts, cigarette trousers or even a complete suit. If you work in a relaxed environment, you can also use them to turn your jeans into something more professional looking.

2. Sexy ankle boots

Distinguish yourself at a party by wearing your cropped trousers or cocktail dress with something other than pumps or sandals. Sexy ankle boots also look amazing with skinny jeans and something oversize, boyish or rock on top.

3. Sexy long boots

Never figured out how to wear midi-length dresses and skirts without looking frumpy? Go for high-leg boots with square or stiletto heels. They will work, no matter whether it is a pencil skirt or a flowy one.

Sneakers

For decades, there was a myth that *les Parisiennes* were oh so elegant they did not succumb to the appeal of sneakers. That's obviously a lie – since the Eighties, sneakers have been invading our streets and wardrobes. We overdosed on them in 2014 during the "Stan Smith peak". Since what *les Parisiennes* do most is walk (our secret to staying thin, remember), even the chicest loafers can't compete with good sneakers.

How to choose them

It is always useful to own a pair of basic, timeless sneakers. Pick them in a neutral colour and a neutral shape. Below-the-ankle models are way easier to match with outfits than higher versions.

You could own one warm leather pair and one light cotton summer pair (in France we have our own local brand called *les Bensimon* – Inès de la Fressange and Jane Birkin are fans).

Then, as always, if you are into sneakers, vary the colours and fabrics. The eccentric shapes usually feel very sporty or edgy, which is not the timeless, quirky Parisian style we are discussing here. However, beware of edgy sneaker trends, which pass as quickly as they appear, leaving you stuck with a pair that already feels outdated.

Timeless sneakers
• Converse Chuck Taylor
• Bensimon
• Adidas Gazelle
• Adidas Stan Smith
• New Balance

"Even the chicest loafers can't compete with good sneakers"

How to wear them

Nowadays, you can wear clean sneakers on casual days as well as in relaxed offices. Have fun and wear your sneakers:

- To dress down a work outfit, such as tailored trousers, a pencil skirt, a work dress, a suit…
- With any casual cropped trousers.
- With sexy mini dresses and skirts.
- To take the girlishness out of a romantic dress.

Statement Pieces

There is nothing wrong with spending your life dressed in timeless wardrobe staples… Chosen wisely and spiced up with colours, prints and accessories, they are enough to create interesting outfits.

But if you want to step up to the next level of style, you need some statement pieces in your wardrobe. By statement pieces I mean pieces of clothing that are so unique they will be noticed by everyone.

To qualify as such they should have either an unusual cut/shape or a colour/print/fabric that really stands out. Or both!

The danger with some statement designer pieces is that their style may become outdated…Therefore, I recommend you avoid buying "the thing of the moment". Instead, try to wander off the beaten track to find a lesser-known designer item that'll successfully pass the test of time.

Style tip

Statement pieces are the reason you need timeless basics to mix them with. You'll always be able to wear a multicoloured, pearl-embellished, embroidered jacket if you own a white T-shirt and a pair of jeans in a neutral colour.

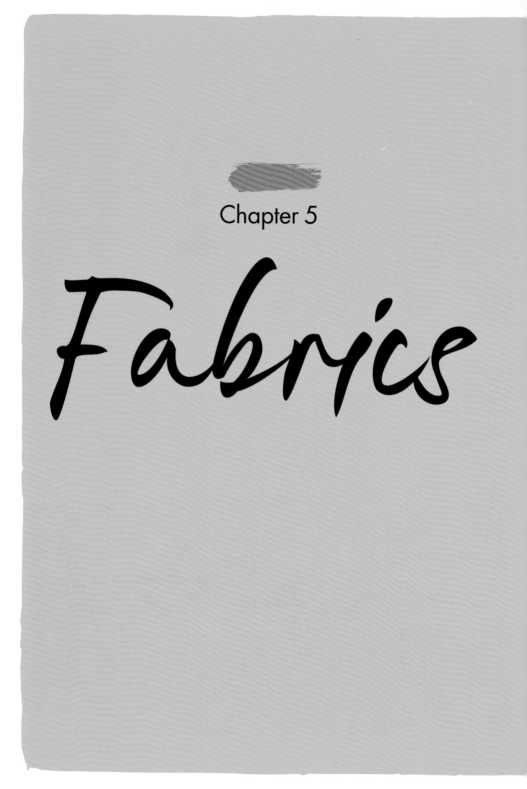

Chapter 5

Fabrics

The Parisian Approach to Fabrics

Les Parisiennes are all about looking sophisticated and wearing good fabrics. For us, the feel of a piece of cloth is almost as important as its look…However, the task of dressing in quality fabrics is becoming more and more difficult to achieve.

Since the year 2000, fabric quality hasn't stopped declining due to the domination of the industry by fast-fashion companies whose aim is to produce fashionable pieces for the minimum possible cost. The first areas to see a drop in quality due to budget cuts were definitely manufacturing and fabric. Unfortunately, high-end brands have followed the same route, putting more money into design and marketing than into the clothes themselves, leading to a significant decrease in the overall quality. This has even been the case in some luxury fashion houses. I once worked as a salesperson for a luxury brand (which I won't name) that sold polyester items made in China for tremendous prices.

So, if not by the price, how can you recognize a good fabric nowadays?

"The feel of a piece of cloth is almost as important as its look"

Fabric Options

Each fabric conveys a certain style. So, just as you would with colour, print or shape, choose a fabric according to the tone you want to give to your outfit. Let's look at four key fabric compositions:

1. Vegetal or natural fabrics

These are all plus points. You can't really go wrong with 100 per cent linen or cotton. Viscose, made of 90 per cent wood, is often a good choice. Be aware that there are different qualities of cotton, not all are equal and it can be worth investing in cloths made with long vegetal fibres.

2. Animal fabrics

Good choices, depending on your convictions. Wool and silk will keep you warm and be long-lasting. View these as an investment because cheap versions usually mean low-quality fabrics and poor animal treatment. None is really cruelty-free but angora and fur are definitely the worst industries. Leather also lasts a long time and ages well.

3. Synthetic fabrics

These are mostly cheap, and look it, but some can be high-end and super-hard-wearing. The only way to tell whether the fabric is good or not is to touch it and look at it closely. Some high-end polyester fabrics look extremely silky and have the advantage of not being as fragile as their natural counterparts. Those fibres are also a good choice if you are vegan and want precious-looking clothes. I recommend you avoid acrylic for knits because it pills and looks super-cheap.

4. Blended fabrics

Blends are not evil. First of all, they often comprise a mix of two good and complementary fabrics. A cashmere-and-silk blend produces light, warm, long-lasting and pill-free garments; a wool-and-cotton blend feels soft and is more robust; a cotton-and-linen mix combines the clean, crisp look of cotton with the raw aspect of linen, for the better. The downside is that these blended fabrics are tougher to recycle.

Synthetic fibres are included in many blends in order to lower the costs. But in some, their characteristics are used to enhance the overall quality of the fabric. For instance, polyester is used to make clothes easier to iron and be more hard-wearing. Although I always prefer 100 per cent natural fabrics, the presence of synthetics in a blend is not always a bad thing.

Look and feel

You cannot really tell the quality of a fabric from just its composition or a picture on the internet. You need to go into the store to look at it and feel it.

Assessing the look and feel of a fabric

- Does it have structure?
Try folding it and see if it goes back to its previous shape. Also notice if it wrinkles (good to know if you're allergic to ironing).
- It is fluid enough?
Make it move and see how it behaves.
- Will it pill?
If it is going to, it has probably done so a little already: check under the armpits.

- Does it shine the way you want?
Some fabrics are intentionally shiny or glowing but others are not supposed to shine at all. If they do, it's proof that they contain polyamide or polyester. Check under a good light to verify that the top or pair of jeans that look natural don't have a synthetic shine to them.
- Is it see-through?
Hold it up in the daylight first and then try it on to double-check.
- Is it loose?
You need to try it on. Make sure the clothes don't "grip" and cling to your body.

Clean Fabrics

For me, "clean" fabrics are those that could be described as pure, fresh, crisp, modern or all of the above. They are free from "imperfections" and their surface is generally smooth, although could have a regular, geometric-looking texture. They may be tight, structured or fluid. These fabrics confer a sense of minimalism to outfits, especially when chosen in pale neutrals.

Top eight clean fabrics

1. Tight cotton jersey
2. Refined cotton canvas
3. Polyester crepe
4. Structured synthetics
5. Perfectly polished white leather
6. Plastics
7. Unmarked denim
8. Ultra-smooth leather

How to wear them

• Clean fabrics are perfect for casual, workwear or sportswear styles.
• Use a crisp, white, heavy cotton jersey T-shirt or shirt to dress up denims, a linen skirt or leather trousers.
• These fabrics are an excellent choice for light yet structured dresses or trousers for spring and summer.

IngridBrochard

Age 40, founder of clothing hire brand Panoply

From Ingrid's window, you can see over the roofs and green gardens of the very chic sixteenth arrondissement. Inside the apartment, the atmosphere is elegant and minimalist. Carefully selected designer pieces are displayed with taste in between the white arches that separate the rooms.

How would you describe your style?
Sober, chic, romantic with a rock twist.

Do you have an iconic piece?
My Saint Laurent tuxedo jacket. I wear it over a dress, with jeans or with the matching trousers, and it always has a great effect. I love the masculine twist about it.

What piece have you owned the longest?
For me, having style is to be a collector. I have always bought quality pieces and keep everything. I own a Balmain dress from the Eighties that used to belong to my grandmother, which I wear with sandals in Ibiza. Vintage pieces are what make your style unique.

Do you dress differently depending on the occasion?
Yes, on a daily basis I wear flats to be comfortable – I move a lot with my job. When there is a special evening, I fancy being more feminine, to seduce, be a *femme fatale* (smiles). I would wear dresses and emphasize my makeup with smoky eyes; but never lipstick or nail polish.

Could you share any style tips?
I love either sober or eccentric garments. The trick is to find balance by matching them together. I am not much of a mix-and-match kind of woman. It is difficult to master, even though I acknowledge some girls look great in it. Yes, that's what I do: one eye-catching item and the rest remain understated. So another of my tips would be to buy less but invest in beautiful pieces you'll keep forever, whether timeless or arty.

How does clothes rental relate to your style philosophy?
We are all victims of impulsive buying and soon after feel unsure about our decision. Being able to pick pieces with a complete sense of freedom pushes us to experience fashion differently. Not having to keep pieces hidden in our wardrobe allows us to become a woman with different façades. Hiring clothes allows us to evoke that feeling of confidence and pleasure we get when wearing a new piece, it's about experience.

How would you describe the style of *la Parisienne*?
During the daytime she may wear jeans and sneakers, and be more chic in the evening. She always accessorizes in order not to look ordinary. I am a bit sad that we tend to dress up less. Maybe we do not have time any more. *La Parisienne*, once she has found her style, is very faithful to it. That's good because it means she is independent and does not get influenced by any trends. But I think she should sometimes dare more.

Raw & Vintage Fabrics

Raw fabrics are the ones that feature imperfection. Perhaps the irregularity of the natural fibre or material is visible in the final cloth, or a piece appears washed-out or used.

The best way to acquire such fabrics is to look for natural fibres and materials that are unprocessed or search for gems in vintage stores. A faux-worn effect will never ever look as good as the real thing. You can find this type of cloth made of linen, cotton (such as denims) or leather, for instance.

Since a natural look and heritage are two things *les Parisiennes* value, they cherish these fabrics. Ask a *Parisienne* how she got the aged patina on her Vuitton bag or the graceful faded lines on her jeans (not the ones on her face) and she'll tell you she inherited the first from her grandma and has owned the second since high school. Which, even if untrue, is a charming story. If you aren't lucky enough to have a Vuitton-loving grandma or have tripled in size since high school, there are thrift stores galore to fulfil all your vintage wishes. Alternatively, be patient; your clothes will age soon enough.

Top six raw fabrics and how to wear them

1. Linen
2. Raw silk
3. Denim
4. Leather
5. Corduroy
6. Chunky knitted wool

Top six vintage finds

1. Leather bag, belt or boots with a patina
2. Denim jeans and jackets with genuine age lines and even some holes
3. Ultra-thin T-shirts on the brink of ripping
4. Graphic T-shirts with faded prints
5. Washed-out, formerly black (now greyish) jeans
6. Worn-in, dirty sneakers (stylishly dirty, not back-from-the-forest dirty)

Faux-worn clothes to avoid

• Fake misplaced holes on jeans or T-shirts. Come on, would you ever create a hole there? You're better off buying something old that is (probably) cheaper and genuine.

• Fake ageing lines on jeans. They never look natural, which is why the French clothing industry nicknamed them "moustaches". In addition, their creation process is damaging for both the environment and workers.

• Fake ageing on leather, which is achieved by applying different shades of polish in a very artificial manner.

Precious Fabrics

I define a fabric as "precious" when it has a princess vibe. It should look rich, sultry and delicate. Of course, if you want the real thing, you will have to spend the corresponding price, but you can quite easily fake it.

These fabrics mostly have some shine to them and may be embellished – the perfect choice for *Parisiennes* who want to look sophisticated by day or night.

You can use a precious fabric to add sophistication to casual outfits that contain clean or raw fabrics (*see* pages 140 and 144).

Top four precious fabrics

1. Satin: slippery and thin
2. Velvet: soft
3. Brocade: stiff
4. Mousseline: see-through and super-light
(Note that these fabrics are all based on silk or silk-lookalike fibres.)

How to wear them

- A silky kimono worn over boyfriend jeans, a vintage leather belt, linen top and a pair of Converse sneakers.
- A yellow velvet mini dress worn with camel leather ankle boots and a beige trench coat.
- Gold-and-black brocade cigarette trousers with black court shoes/pumps and a crisp white shirt.
- A mousseline midi skirt with an oversize knit and high-leg boots.

Chapter 6
Accessories

The Parisian Approach to Accessories

Since a Parisian's wardrobe staples are timeless items, you definitely want to spice them up in order to stand out from the crowd. For that purpose, there is nothing better than accessories, which is why *les Parisiennes* cherish their jewellery, scarves, shoes and bags just as much as their clothes.

The usually rather classic *Parisiennes* tend to be much more daring when shopping for accessories. It is common to meet women who have a wardrobe full of classic clothing next to a shoe collection that would make Carrie Bradshaw jealous.

There are two types of accessories. The ones you do not really notice, since they blend into your outfit, and the ones that really stand out, making a statement by themselves. *La Parisienne* definitely likes both, although she may be more drawn to one than the other, for example preferring to be discreet with jewellery and eccentric with shoes.

"Les Parisiennes cherish their jewellery, scarves, shoes and bags just as much as their clothes"

Scarves

When it gets a bit chilly in Paris, everyone puts their scarves on, whether in the cold of winter or just on a breezy summers evening. Scarves are so important to us that we have different names for them, and each has a different use and style. Let me introduce them.

Scarf styles

1. *Le foulard*
The light scarf
For when it is not too cold. *Le foulard* is made of a light fabric, such as cotton, linen, viscose or silk. Its size varies from tiny to extra-large. The classics are rather broad and long so that you can wrap them around your neck without too much thought. I would avoid the long, skinny ones. Choose a fabric that is easy to "fluff" and arrange, but loose enough to hang in a cool manner.

How to wear it
Hold up your scarf by one corner (so that it creates a pointy shape rather than a horizontal line at the hem) and drape it around your neck. Position it so that the ends hang at the front somewhere above your hips and below your breasts. Casually wrap the ends of the scarf around your neck while "fluffing" it out to create fullness.

2. *Le carré*
The square scarf

I am not being honest in giving this scarf its own category since it is also a *foulard*. As its names indicates, it has a square shape that can vary from small to very large. It is made of twill silk or its lookalike, or even a rather stiff cotton canvas. Since the small ones can look rather conservative, I recommend you wear them with cool clothes. The big ones look very casual.

How to wear it
If using a big *carré*, fold it in half to create a large triangle. Hold the triangle in front of you with the long, straight edge at the top. Cross the two ends at the back of your neck and then let them hang in front, on either side of the triangle. If it is a tiny *carré*, you could fold it the same way and tie it at the back so that it is super-close to your neck, like a necktie.

3. *L'étole*
The shoulder scarf

Some may think this quite old-fashioned, but it is considered a dressy item and is still used for ceremonies. *L'étole* is very wide and rather short so you don't have to roll it or tie it.

How to wear it
Put it around your shoulders. Period.

4. *L'écharpe*
The winter scarf

Made of wool or cashmere, this scarf is usually long and large.

How to wear it
Drape the scarf around your neck and position it so that the ends hang at the front somewhere above your hips and below your breasts. Wrap both ends of the scarf around your neck, leaving space for your chin (you do not want to look as though you are being strangled). Adjust the two ends so that they hang at the front almost (but not exactly) level with each other.

Style tip

For a long and lean silhouette, simply drape a scarf around your neck and let the ends hang at the front.

Belts

Now that you have decided whether it is a good idea to belt or not to belt (*see* pages 90–1), let's focus on what you are going to belt your outfits with. Belts are great accessories that enable you to add texture, colour or ornamentation to the centre of your outfit.

Types of belt

Did you know that most belts were designed for a specific use or position on the body? Pick the one that will work with your outfit.

Jeans belt
These are designed to fit precisely into the belt loops of a pair of jeans. So if you have jeans to belt, don't make the mistake of using the tiny belts that are meant for suit trousers.

Narrow belts
Thinner belts are classier and will be perfect on dresses or work trousers. They may be worn high or low.

Wide belts
Large belts really underline the shape of the body, whether it is the waist (corset-style) or the hips (not so fashionable at the moment, I must admit). They can appear very sexy and even couture on a dress. Sometimes they have a buckle, sometimes you have to knot them. Large belts are definitely statement accessories, no matter how discreet their colour.

"A vintage belt in a natural leather is perfect to wear with jeans"

Belt styles

A belt conveys
a style through its
fabric, colour,
print and buckle.
Choose it according
to your outfit.

Raw

A vintage belt in
natural leather that
has already had
years of wear, or a
new one that you will
mould to your own
body, ideally with a
discreet brass buckle,
is perfect to wear with
jeans, flowery dresses
or natural "imperfect"
fabrics (see page 144).

Dressy

The tiny patent leather
belt you wear with a
trouser suit or the thin
gold or silver belt you
use on a dressy dress.

Funky

A belt that will make
a style statement and
spice up a classic outfit.
It could be brightly
coloured, printed
(leopard or zebra, for
instance) or sparkly.

Boho

For example, braided
leather or ribbon that
you wrap around
your waist and tie
in a knot will add
some bohemian
sophistication to your
jeans and fluid dresses.
The knotted belt is
meant to be worn
high-waisted on a
dress, with one end
hanging down freely.

Ornamental buckle

The buckle will be like
a jewel on your belly.
It can be tiny or big, in
any style. Perfect with
a basic dress or jeans-
and-shirt outfit.

Bags

In a perfect world, there would be a bag for every occasion, perfectly matching your outfit and containing everything you need. In real life, most of us use the same bag almost every day, except when we suddenly swap it in a rush for another one, because it really doesn't match, and forget to pack essential things (*le métro* pass, of course).

There are a number of reasons for not owning many day bags: it is a pain to transfer the contents from one to another, they are pricey, they take up room in your crowded closet, you actually do not really need to own more than two…It is easier to have a little collection of tiny evening bags for occasions, as do most *Parisiennes*… unless they prefer to carry their keys, lipstick, phone and credit card in their pockets.

If you were to have a capsule wardrobe of bags, here are the ones that would be the most useful…

A capsule wardrobe

The everyday handbag
This should be able to hold everything you need on a daily basis. Since you are going to take it everywhere, it should be hard-wearing and have comfortable straps (not too small, too thin or painful). Do not pick a bag that is too big for your own size.

A dark neutral colour (black or natural leather being must-haves) will be easier to match. Choose your shade according to your wardrobe. Brown tends to look casual, vintage or bohemian; black feels more chic.

Already own the basics? Add some coloured versions to your collection. But remember: since this is probably an item you are going to keep for many years, you may get bored of something that is too eccentric.

The hangout handbag
When you don't need the whole package but still plan to spend the afternoon out, you need a medium-sized day bag, which should be comfortable and versatile. You could own one in a neutral colour and a more fun one in a different colour or a pattern.

The party handbag
For when you want your bag to be as dressy as you are. Again, a neutral one is useful, to ensure you have a match for your craziest dresses. In this case, silver or gold could be your neutrals. Then have fun! There are all sorts of shapes, fabrics, colours and ornamentations to experiment with. It could be like carrying a little piece of art in your hand.

The everyday summer bag
Because there are days when it feels too warm for your (probably dark leather) everyday bag and you need a lighter version. Opt for a softer colour and a lighter fabric, such as canvas.

The holiday bag
This one can be just a cotton tote, a straw bag or an ethnic bag… What matters most is that it cuts you off from the professional world and matches your summer outfits. It would feel weird to mix a dressy black leather bag with a flowy summer dress, wouldn't it?

Style tip
Try a light "bag inside the bag" containing all your essentials in order to transfer them easily from one bag to another.

Shoes & Hosiery

We have already discussed shoes in "Wardrobe Essentials" (*see* pages 124–31), but there we only talked about the basics. Shoes can, however, be a wonderful style-changing accessory. Tights (pantyhose) may be the cheapest and most efficient way to accessorize an outfit. And socks are a subtle alternative.

Why invest in statement shoes?
• If they are like a piece of art, they will be timeless.
• Your feet will most likely remain the same size so you can consider them a good investment.
• You'll be able to mix them with plenty of different outfits.

Here are a few things you could look into when shopping for statement shoes:

Statement shoes

Colour
Start with classic shapes in daring shades but do not be afraid of shoes that feature several colours: you'll be able to match them with neutrals as well as with any colour featured in the shoe.

Unusual heel or sole
The heel of the shoe could be gold, transparent, bejewelled, coloured… And so could the sole.

Ornamentation
Be bold and try pompoms, crystal inserts, embroidery… It doesn't have to be loud. The subtlety of the cat-faced loafer has enabled it to become a classic.

Fabric
Try faux-pony skin, metallics, snakeskin pattern, patent leather or a fabric mix.

Print
Leopard, zebra, tropical plants, flowers…

Hosiery

As essential to us as butter. Indeed, the tights (pantyhose) and socks section stands right in the middle of the ground floor of Monoprix (our semi-fancy corner supermarket). Think like a *Parisienne* and use them to pimp up your dresses, skirts…

My favourite socks

Sparkly
The ideal way to spice up the space in between your brogues and your cropped trousers. You could also wear them on top of your black tights (pantyhose), so they show just above your ankle boots.

Plumetis
Perfect for giving your low masculine shoes a girly edge. Or to warm up your court shoes and sandals in winter.

Fishnet
A hint of sexiness somewhere between your low boyish shoes and your trousers. Also they look darling with sandals or court shoes.

Printed
Whether you opt for elegant dots or refined plaid, play it like a dandy and let them show with your low leather shoes.

My favourite tights (pantyhose)

Black opaque and semi-opaque
Always own a few pairs of these. They are perfectly versatile and look professional. Swap for dark brown when composing an outfit of warm tones, to avoid a harsh contrast.

Plumetis
Those little dots on a sheer background are adorably flirty. In black they'll match every colour or print. Go for a coloured version, if you can find them.

Lace
So refined! Unlease their full potential and match them with a plain colour.

Back-seamed
The sexiest of all designs looks amazing with midi-length dresses and skirts.

Coloured
All eyes will be on your legs. Bored of your LBD? Go red!

Hats & Gloves

In the past, it was unconventional for a woman to go out "*en cheveux*" (meaning "in hair"), as opposed to in a hat or headscarf, and gloves were a symbol of elegance. Nowadays, wearing a hat is so unusual it makes you stand out from the crowd and we merely consider gloves our allies to fight the cold. For me, a hat is the most daring of all accessories, and function and elegance can go hand in hand (or hand in glove).

Choosing hats

The beanie
Depending on the shape of your face, choose one that is small and tight or loose and puffy. With its casual and sporty look, it is an easy accessory that can be chosen in lively colours to spice up a winter outfit. Always make sure there is a little hair showing at the front or sides to frame your face. You can wear your beanie very slightly to the side for a careless effect (even if you do actually care).

The turban
The turban can be worn both for day or night, if you choose it in a fancy fabric. As it is very fitted, you can use statement earrings to balance the "little head" effect. Traditionally, you are supposed to hide your hair inside. However, you could let your fringe out by pulling

the turban further back on your head, or let your long hair hang down at the sides.

The classic hat

Hats such as fedoras or capelines (soft felt hats with wide floppy brims) have a very sophisticated feel and can therefore be difficult to wear. My advice would be to style it in a relaxed manner, as if it were a normal thing to wear. In a nutshell, don't pull out the full "Instagrammer on a photoshoot" style, just because you are sporting a hat. With either the capeline or fedora, long hair worn loose is perfect. As fedoras can feel a little more boyish, you can also try hiding your hair inside the hat.

The straw hat

Whether it is a *canotier* ("boater") or a wide-brimmed straw hat, this is the perfect accompaniment to your holiday outfits and will protect you from the sun in a chic manner. The more opaque and densely woven the hat, the more protected you'll be. You can let your hair hang free, braid it or hide it inside the hat with just a few loose strands around your face.

The beret

This iconic French hat is making a comeback. And there is a very specific way to style it. First, make sure it is puffed out all around your head, then pull it sideways.

The scarf

Bad hair day? Looking to add some colour to your look? Roll up a little scarf and tie it in your hair as an accessory. (You can buy ones with ready-made knots if you feel a bit lazy.)

Choosing gloves

Fabric

Most gloves on the market are made of wool. They can be warm and fun but have a plump-fingers effect that will not look chic. To get elegant gloves that give you long and lean fingers, you need to go to a specialist store where you'll have your hands measured before being offered your precise size. Unfortunately for the cold-sensitive, the prettiest gloves are made of thin leather. Opt for some lining inside if you want real cold protection.

Colour and print

I recommend you go for the basics before you get the crazy stuff. But if you already KNOW that your coats are black and beige, that you own plenty of neutral shoes and scarves, then why not dare choose some more eccentric gloves right at the outset? How about leopard-print or burgundy ones? Or a pair of fun wool gloves featuring a print?

Style tip: fingerless gloves

They are not only for Madonna and can be very useful when you need to use your fingers – especially if you can't handle staying off your phone. Plus, you get to display your winter manicure.

Cécile Fricker Lehanneu

Age 43, stylist and founder of fine jewellery brand Cécil

Next to Montparnasse, Cécile's classic, spacious Haussmannian apartment is filled with tastefully curated unusual pieces of furniture and art. She greets me with a cup of fine tea served in ravishing handmade non-matching cups.

How would you describe your style?
I don't really think about it. Maybe something about being feminine…but not everyday. And elegant. The way I assemble clothes is what makes me look unique. And it's something I enjoy a lot, as I am a stylist.

Did your style evolve over the years?
I'm not afraid to be feminine, glamorous even. My style has always been kind of edgy: I have been collecting beautiful pieces since I was 20 years old.

Does your style change according to the occasion?
Yes. For evenings, I really like to pull out wow-factor outfits, very couture, with precious fabrics and heels. For daytime, I aim for comfortable mixes that suit my life as a mum.

Do you follow trends?
I love prints and fun cuts so, yes, I do happen to buy pieces that are "in" but only because I love them, not just to follow a trend. That means I don't stop wearing them when the trend is over.

What about makeup?
I wear very little. I like some foundation to protect my delicate skin and cover dark circles, some mascara and blush to be fresh-faced, and that's about it. At night I'll pull out bright red or pink lipstick.

What's your relationship with jewellery?
Jewels are the king of objects. They are the ones that stay, the ones you pass on. I have been fascinated by precious stones since I was a child. Choosing and wearing them is a question of intuition. Creating them, too. For my own line, Cécil, I want them to be precious, romantic and modern.

What piece has been in your closet the longest?
I started wearing Japanese designs when I was 21 and have kept them all. They are so timeless.

Some style advice?
Know yourself. Always buy what pleases you and not others. And know what suits your body and complexion: never go against them. When you know how to make yourself look beautiful, everything is possible. Oh, and when I buy a piece of clothing, I always picture what I'll wear it with. I choose what will work with my existing wardrobe. I think that's a good tip, too.

What do you think makes French women so stylish?
They own a lot of basic wardrobe staples, which enable them to wear anything.

Jewellery

Jewellery is the ultimate accessory because its sole purpose is to decorate you. It is essential if you are trying to create a style.

No need to go big. There are two different kinds of jewellery: *les bijoux de peau et les gros bijoux*. The first translates as "skin jewellery", or jewels that are so fine it feels as though they are part of the skin. The second is the famous "statement jewellery".

Some women are only attracted to one kind; some like both. If you are not yet familiar with accessorizing with jewellery, I suggest you build up a collection comprising a mix of both kinds, like Jane Birkin, a renowned French style icon who is always pictured wearing simple outfits with one piece of jewellery, which is sometimes very delicate and at other times quite daring.

Les bijoux de peau

These are the pieces you'll sleep in, make love in, shower in…Even the tiniest necklace can make the simplest outfit look precious. Invest in these pieces – you want them to last you a lifetime. They could be birthday presents to yourself, gifts from your loved ones or family heirlooms. They should be entirely yours, so have them custom-made if you wish.

You could have one delicate piece of each type of jewellery: a necklace so fine you can just see it shine on your skin, earrings so dainty you can wear them with everything, a bracelet that glides silently around your wrist and maybe one or several rings.

The only problem when you own something delicate and precious is that it is difficult to wear it too close to some types of costume jewellery. Wearing real gold and diamonds next to Swarovksi crystals and gold-plated silver can make the latter look very cheap, even though they are not per se. So if you have one very precious ring set with diamonds, the more modest ones may have to migrate to your other hand. Or leave your precious ring in its box from time to time.

Gros bijoux

Unless you are Marie Antoinette, opt for costume jewellery – voluminous pieces made of semi-precious materials and non-noble metals. It could be made of natural stones, brass or even methacrylate (a smooth ivory-like synthetic).

Be daring and make a real statement with your jewellery. Perhaps earrings that hang beneath your jaw line, a necklace that you notice before the dress, or a bracelet that clangs when you put your arm on the table.

Do not overthink when buying these pieces; you'll always find clothes simple enough to match them with. What's important is that you have a real crush on them.

What jewellery goes together?

In the Fifties, women used to wear matching sets of jewellery. While this is considered old-fashioned nowadays, unfortunately, not all jewellery works well when mixed together. To avoid a *faux pas*, go for different pieces of jewellery that are of a similar style. What would you think of baroque earrings next to a minimal necklace? Or a smooth architectural ring next to an irregular handmade bracelet? Strange, isn't it?

Layering jewellery

- *Les bijoux de peau*
Try adorning your ears with plenty of mini gold hoops and studs, and your wrists, neck and fingers with myriad super-fine gold bracelets, necklaces and rings. The style of each piece can be slightly different: a thin bohemian ring worn with something more minimal, for example.

- *Gros bijoux*
Be careful about how many you put together. A statement necklace and statement earrings next to each other are often too much (lose the earrings and go for tiny studs instead). Several chunky rings can also be too much. Wear fewer or wear your statement ring on one hand and several delicate ones on the other. A big bracelet or cuff is a good match for a statement ring.

Style tips:

- Use brooches and pins to customize your clothes. Pin a jewel on the collar of your coat, on your sweater, cardigan, scarf, hat or even your T-shirt.
- There is nothing wrong with mixing gold and silver.

Styling jewellery *and* clothes

Consider the overall style of your outfit, then focus on the area of clothing that will be next to the piece of jewellery you are about to put on (the neckline for necklaces and earrings, and the cuff of sleeves for bracelets). You can either match the style of your clothes and jewellery or go for a clash:
• Clean, timeless clothes with arty, imperfect-looking jewellery
• Sporty or rock clothes with baroque jewellery
• Edgy, minimal clothes with ethnic jewellery

How to accessorize your clothes

• **Busy necklines**
If your top is ornamented around the neck, has ruffles, a Victorian collar or visible buttons, it is easier to skip the necklace and opt for earrings instead.

• **Turtlenecks**
Perfect with just oversize earrings. Long chains and pendants are currently quite outdated but will surely make a comeback and they are also a good match.

• **V-necks**
It is very pretty to wear a thin delicate necklace against your skin, whether it is a short pendant, chain or a choker, or a longer and heavier V-shaped pendant.

• **Crew necks**
Statement necklaces, such as chokers or rather short rounded ones work well with crew necks. You could also try long V-shaped pendants, either thin or chunky.

• **Button-up collars**
If you wear your collars open, they are like V-necks; if you do the buttons up, you can add round statement necklaces.

• **Narrow sleeves**
You could top bodycon sleeves with chunky cuffs or bracelets.

• **Wide sleeves**
Either opt for rings or roll your sleeves up to show some skin (and some bracelets).

Glasses

Whether they are there to protect you from the sun, shield you from your many, many fans or help you see or read, glasses surely will change the features of your face. Take your time to choose them wisely.

Prescription glasses

Since you are going to see them on your nose on a daily basis, they'd better be a good catch. You do not want them to annoy you when you are composing outfits, so I suggest you choose a neutral frame. Black is always a good option for dark-haired people but may harden the faces of brunettes with warm undertones and make blue eyes appear as cold as steel. If you are aiming for something chic and softer, tortoiseshell frames should fit the bill. You could also opt for vintage metallic frames in gold, rose gold or silver shades. If you are a blonde with pale skin, transparent, grey or nude acetate frames will blend in with your complexion and hair colour.

I advise everyone to avoid the "no-frame" styles. You'll still notice the frame but will lose the style. That's a lose-lose situation. Regarding the shape, I recommend you stay rather classic, even if you opt for big statement glasses. Eccentric models will be difficult to match with other items and you may get bored of them. Please forget about meaningless details such as flower embellishments on the arms or little gems that will add nothing but complication to your morning routine.

If you have opted for metallic frames, avoid wearing metallic earrings and piercings that will give you a "full metal face", like when you were 15 with braces.

Sunglasses

The bigger, the better! As long as they are not wider than your face, making you resemble a bee, you'll definitely get more protection with wide glasses. Plus they are more chic. Have you ever seen a movie star sporting small sunglasses?

If you live in Western Europe and aren't trying to hide (cue Karl Lagerfeld), sunglasses are a seasonal thing that you do not wear inside. You can be a little eccentric in your choice. Why not go for a bold colour or a white frame? Of course, black and brown are the safest colours for composing outfits, but what about a crazy shape such as outrageous cat's eyes or baroque arms?

Makeup

There are two ways to use makeup. Either to enhance your natural beauty in a manner that no one notices (well, no MAN, but the trained eyes of women will know). Apply some foundation, concealer, highlighter and blush to even out your skin tone, diminish your dark circles and get a natural-looking glow. Or you can use makeup as an accessory to contrast or underline the style of clothes you are wearing. Lipsticks, eyeliners and eyeshadows are one of the cheapest ways to impact your style. This "statement makeup" is the topic I will talk about as a stylist. The rest is the domain of a makeup artist.

Disclaimer: The tips that I am going to give may seem complicated to some but they are essentially entry-level makeup tricks. Use YouTube tutorials to get step-by-step instructions but not from a Kardashian lookalike. Instead try French makeup artist Violette or Lisa Eldridge.

Eyeliner

The cat's-eye flick is like a signature to your face. In black, it suits almost all eyes, giving them definition and a sexy almond shape. You could pair it with bold red lips in a pin-up manner or just go for lip balm for a Sixties vibe.

Dare to try colours or metallics (shine will really get your eyes sparkling). Since the line you draw is thin, it will create a wonderful impact without looking as eccentric as you might think (*see picture opposite*).

Mascara

If you like the fresh, innocent Sixties style, try overloading your lashes with mascara with the rest of your face kept bare, except for some peachy rosy blush.

Smoky eye

The smoky eye creates a very intense gaze, which is either very sophisticated or rock, depending on your hairstyle, the way you are dressed and how smudged the makeup is. An excellent choice for parties, it goes with both bare lips or a sultry pout.

Lipstick

The secret weapon of *les Parisiennes*.
Red lips on a bare (or bare-looking) face
is a Parisian classic that will save any sad
outfit from boredom. Plus you don't need
more makeup than this to get a natural,
fresh glow. For the optimum effect, pick
the shade(s) of red that suits you best
with the help of a makeup artist.

Nails

Les Parisiennes are not hugely into long
talons and fussy manicures. Clean and
short red nails are one of their favourite
styles because you can do it yourself and
it is super-versatile. If you feel like a
change, try unusual colours: midnight
blue, pastel lilac, copper and so on…And
for an occasion, go to the salon and try a
sophisticated manicure. Why not try a half-
moon manicure on almond-shaped nails?

Colours on the eyes

Dare to try unusual
colours, which will
be noticed but won't
look as eccentric
as you might think.
Pick a shade that will
enhance the beauty
of your eyes. Try
purple and red for
hazel eyes; copper
and silver for blue
eyes; dark pinks and
reds for green eyes.
If you have very dark
skin, try electric blue
or green (they work
wonders as eyeliner).

Chapter 7

Styles

The Many Styles of les Parisiennes

In this chapter I have identified what I consider to be the five main style families in Paris: the not-so classics, the dressy bohemians, the French pin-ups, the arty ladies and the sexy rock chicks.

As *les Parisiennes* have countless style influences, instead of conforming to the codes of a particular style group, the free-spirited *Parisienne* prefers to pick and mix from different influences and put them together on a classic base. When there is a new trend, she incorporates it in her look rather than changing her entire style to conform to it.

Use the following portraits as moodboards to inspire you to create your own Parisian mix-and-match of style influences.

"Create your own Parisian mix-and-match of style influences"

Not-so Classic

Daytime

Bourgeoise but not boring would define this classic *Parisienne* who always adds a twist to her outfits. In her daytime wardrobe you'll find a vast majority of neutrals and timeless staples. As she doesn't like to draw attention to herself, she stays at a safe distance from anything that would be too loud. Yet she is not as boring as one may think and gets bolder when it comes to details and accessories. If you take a closer look, you'll notice her eye-printed shirt, her yellow shoes and oversize ring. Some days she'll swap her neutral basics for coloured alternatives. If she is young, she may go for a timeless black hoodie and pastel pink sneakers under her favourite trench coat.

Dress like this
Parisienne

- Invest in beautiful pieces
- Mix timeless classics with coloured accessories
- Wear delicate jewellery
- Brush your hair, but not too much
- Wear natural makeup
- Keep your nails short and perfectly manicured

Night-time

When night comes, it's all about the fabric and the cut. Each time she shows up at a dressy dinner in one of the many Haussmannian apartments of her friends, she is sporting a different little black dress (along with the same stunning black court shoes). Sometimes the dress is long with a slit, sometimes short with a low back, sometimes covered in lace but always timeless. For a very special occasion, she will opt for a more daring colour and fabric but will stick to an understated cut, as she prefers to be noticed for her discreet elegance.

Dress like this
Parisienne

- Invest in timeless dresses
- Try a black jumpsuit instead of a little black dress
- Dare to pin a brooch on your cashmere sweater

Dressy Bohemian

Daytime

Even though she is working in advertising, this *Parisienne* wishes she were a musician on the road, a dandy poetess or a bohemian painter. As it feels too late for a career change, at least she has the opportunity to get the look.

Her style influences come from all around the world. She is able to mix an Indian bag, a Native American belt and English brogues in the same outfit. She also time-travels, scouring vintage stores to find the perfect Victorian collar along with the best Eighties second-hand Levi's. She likes everything that has a patina, flowy clothes and precious details such as embroidery, fringes or lace inserts.

She often goes to boutiques in Le Marais that are entirely dedicated to her bohemian sophistication, featuring linen, velvet, precious silks, raw jeans, dark, muted colours and faded prints.

Dress like this
Parisienne

- Combine raw and precious fabrics
- Wear prints and mix them
- Add embroidery, pearls, feathers or fringes to your outfits
- Pretend you never brush your hair or go to the hairdresser (but use conditioner and a comb)
- Wear flowy items
- Overload on jewellery
- Wear scarves
- Layer

Night-time

When night comes, the bohemian *Parisienne* hangs out in the coolest dirty dive bars of Paris or on a friend's Persian carpet. Dressed pretty much as she was earlier in the day, she enjoys looking effortless even though putting together her outfit was obviously time consuming. The observant will have noticed that she's taken the time to gather her long hair up into a messy bun, paint smoky eyes or darker lips on her face and change into a low-cut silk top.

Dress like this
Parisienne

- Master the smudged makeup style
- Wear shiny socks with your heels
- Layer your dressy dress with a blazer or a kimono
- Take your old jeans for a dance with a low-cut silk cami and velvet heels
- Wear oversize jewellery

French Pin-up

Daytime

With her shiny hair, rosy cheeks and high heels, she is the French version of the American pin-up. Dresses, retro heels, voluptuous cleavage, dot print, high belts and red lips are her trademarks. Yet she doesn't dress as "basic" as you may think and likes to add variety to her healthy sexiness. One day it will be high-waisted jeans with patent red ballet flats and a flowery short-sleeved shirt; the day after, she'll be seen in a full-length belted blue jumpsuit with gold heels…Colours, sparkles and prints confer an aura of *joie de vivre* to her outfits. Very much into quirky or old-fashioned accessories, she finds her gems in little multi-brand boutiques and vintage stores.

Dress like this
Parisienne

- Define your waist as often as you can
- Contrast flowy and bodycon pieces
- Wear fresh prints
- Platforms, kitten heels and other easy-to-wear heels are your daytime staples
- Wear nail polish on short or almond-shaped nails
- Layer with tight cardigans or belted trench coats
- Give your feet a rest with ballet or pointy flats
- Think Brigitte Bardot

Night-time

When she plans a night out dancing, she picks an outfit that flatters her curves. For the waist, she goes for cinching, belting, a high waist or bodycon; for the feet, she chooses heels that make her bottom look rounder; for the décolletage, low is almost mandatory. A lover of vintage glamour imagery, she's into classic colours such as black, red, nude or white, but may also fall for more unexpected shades and sophisticated prints.

Dress like this
Parisienne

- Wear low-cut, cleavage-revealing or bodycon tops
- Define your waist
- Layer with belted blazers and kimonos
- Wear red lipstick
- Wear winged eyeliner

Emmanuelle Mary

Age 39, entrepreneur (PR and yoga teacher)

Emmanuelle welcomes me into her charming apartment in the lively eighteenth arrondissement. In the living room we are surrounded by shelves topped with CDs, books stacked on an eclectic assemblage of furniture, and art pieces. She shows me her tiny, crowded walk-in closet – well, actually, more of a squeeze-into closet (*c'est Paris!*) – which is full of crazy pieces that seem to come from different places and different eras.

How would you describe your style?
Sexy, rock, natural and "funky".

Can you tell us about how you assembled your outfit for today?
This skirt by Filles à Papa, a Belgian brand, I love; it perfectly embodies my style. It has a sexy shape, a fun print and a refined pink satin layer. Perfect to twist with my AC/DC vintage tee for my rock side. And I always wear plenty of jewellery; it makes everything look so fun.

Do you dress differently according to the occasion?
Yes, but I am always true to my own style. When I have a professional meeting it would be straight with hints of my funky, sexy self. On a day off I would be more eccentric with a straight edge in order to keep the elegance.

What's the oldest garment you own?
(*Emmanuelle pulls out a short flowery sundress.*) I have had this since I was 15 years old.

And you never stopped wearing it?
No, it is one of my summer staples. I actually wore it yesterday paired with biker boots.

And do you have other "closet dinosaurs"?
(*She goes back in the closet and comes out with a Nineties-looking tube dress.*) This is about the same age as the sundress and I wore it recently, too.

But I bet you stopped wearing it for a while, didn't you? (*judging by the style of the dress that has just recently made a comeback.*)
Yes, indeed, at one point the dress was out of style and didn't feel appealing any more so I stopped wearing it, but still loved it… until the Nineties made a comeback, which made me want to wear it again.

What about makeup?
On a daily basis, nothing. I also do not style my hair much: some combing and I'm done. For a special event I would do black smoky eyes and powder blush or bright lips on a bare face. But not the two combined. In the end, it looks effortless.

Could you share some style advice?
For me it is all about freedom of tone. Make your own rules, wear what you enjoy and do not care too much about what you *should* do. It is all about finding the necklace, the blazer, the shoes…that will give your outfit that little "*je ne sais quoi*". Once you own them, just assemble and bam! No need to spend hours pampering yourself in the bathroom. And, most importantly, trust yourself.

Arty

Daytime

You'll meet her at gallery openings or fashion shows. Either super-independent of trends or a dedicated follower of them, the arty girl masters fashion and creates her own style tricks. The "arty" spectrum is very broad and can go from "fashion editor" to "impoverished artist". All share an element of the unexpected that makes heads turn, people stare and street photographers get hysterical. This *Parisienne* definitely dresses to impress. Dramatic cuts, unusual colours, mixed prints and sculptural shoes are her fashion candies. But, hey, as she is still a *Parisienne*, she'll always incorporate a hint of the classics that'll make her approachable instead of otherworldly.

Dress like this *Parisienne*

- Wear designer statement pieces
- Show your master style tricks (half-tucking in, mixing prints and so on)
- Dare to be ironic
- Be unexpected
- Keep your hair down and your makeup low-key

Night-time

To go dancing on a "guest-list-only" Parisian rooftop, the arty *Parisienne* will turn her creativity to night-time dressing. Which typically means the usual night codes adapted to her style: extreme heels, extreme sophistication, extreme makeup and maybe a "hairdo". She'll make sure she stands out from the crowd, wearing a suit when everyone else is in dresses, going for bright prints when the vast majority have opted for black or preferring a short haircut when the others are sporting a hairdo.

If you want to do it the Parisian way, make sure you stand out from the crowd...while blending in. The arty *Parisienne* is not as eccentric as her foreign counterparts and while she likes to be noticed, she doesn't want to look as if she has come in fancy dress. Therefore, she'll still match the dress code...just in her own way.

Dress like this
Parisienne

- Be the only one to look like you
- Wear a "piece of art": a dress, jewellery, a pair of shoes...
- Try a daring hairstyle or makeup: a sharp bob or silver eyelids, for instance

Sexy Rock Chick

Daytime

With her tight clothes, her love for leather and her smoky eyes, the rock chick *Parisienne* is subsequently sexy. But the opposite would be true as well: *la Parisienne* aiming for sexy is always rock (when she is not aiming for the French pin-up style). It's a way of playing by the rules and dabbling in rebellion, of being provocative without being too obvious that pleases Parisians so much. Indeed, they fear the tackiness of being too "in your face" sexy and prefer to be more subtle (which they do very efficiently).

In the daytime, she's into tight jeans, leather trousers, cigarette trousers, mini skirts and bodycon dresses. Most of her wardrobe revolves around black and neutrals and sometimes she'll add pops of red into the mix. Yet if she inserts a sweet shade into her look, she is able to turn it into something rebellious, like that time when she wore a loose pink sweater with her vinyl trousers.

Dress like this
Parisienne

- Make leather, jeans, loose knits and tees your wardrobe staples
- Wear a trench like you don't care
- Your hair should look unkempt
- Whether flat or with heels, you'll have a pair of ankle boots for every occasion
- Wear your shirts largely unbuttoned with the sleeves rolled up
- Wear no makeup or just go for eyes and lips, but the look shouldn't be too polished

Night-time

To meet her friends at a rad birthday party, she may or may not get dressed up. If she doesn't, she'll probably just add makeup or heels, or change her top for one with a lower neckline. If she does, she may sport a little black dress with heels, a black jumpsuit with a big gold belt or a messy hairdo.

Dress like this
Parisienne

- Use black, gold and red at night
- Or burgundy, the colour of wine
- Master the smoky eye make up look

- Layer with blazers or biker jackets
- Do not be afraid to go short
- Or to go low-cut
- Then act like you don't care

Chapter 8

Your Own Kind of Beauty

Dressing for Your Body Type

As French women dress for themselves before thinking of following any trends, they tend to wear fashionable items only if they flatter their silhouette – a behaviour that (strangely) would be considered contrary to the precepts of the positive body-image movement. Indeed, the defenders of this cause advocate that every woman looks beautiful in the same clothing designs, no matter her size. I agree that no one should feel forbidden to wear clothes because of society standards. Nevertheless, claiming that some clothing designs look equally beautiful on every body type is denying that each body is different. Every person has types of clothes that flatter them more than others, and it is not a bad thing if those clothes are not the same for everyone.

Should clothes always be flattering? In my opinion, yes. Clothes are supposed to dress you; you are not supposed to adapt to them. Therefore, the body is the first element you should take into consideration when designing an outfit. You wouldn't randomly put clothes together without paying attention to the way they work with one another, would you? So why would you put clothes on yourself without paying attention to the way they work with your body?

Before brands start to offer clothes for more varied body shapes, you can DIY a silhouette that flatters you the most by choosing and assembling clothes wisely in the stores. In terms of styling, flattering clothes are those that enhance your beauty, creating a harmonious silhouette by revealing some of your best assets.

"Flattering clothes are those that enhance your beauty"

Since all women are unique, it is tricky to classify them into "body types" as most style books do. My clients often come to me and ask what "fruit" they are because they think they have "pear" hips and an "apple" tummy, which makes them a breed that no style book has yet determined how to dress. Since this method isn't clear, my advice centres on body parts. You'll also notice that I have focused on body parts that are "bigger" or "smaller" than the average because dressing gets more difficult when you get outside of the "norm" that clothes are designed for. I have then suggested clothes that would suit you, depending on how you want your body to look.

Above the Waist

Neck & shoulders

In French, we praise a straight neck for giving you a beautiful "*port de tête*". In English, it could be translated as "carrying the head upright or with pride". To achieve a beautiful allure, pay attention to this feature and your posture. Look ahead when you walk – shoulders back, neck straight – as if you were balancing a glass of water on your head, and avoid looking down at your phone.

Long neck

Lucky you, all necklines, jewellery and scarves suit you.
• Low necklines, such as V-necks or scoop necks, are suitable but be aware that they will emphasize the length of your neck.
• Turtlenecks, Victorian collars and all high necklines
• Regular necklines such as shirts and crews
• Dress up the area with jewellery, from large and voluminous earrings (try oversize hoops) to chunky, circle-shaped necklaces and chokers.

Short neck

• Opt for clothes and styles that elongate your neck. This means avoiding high or fussy necklines that can make you look as if you are drowning.
• When tying your scarf, pull it away from your neck so it doesn't make your neck disappear.
• Favour necklaces that sit either in the middle of the chest or lower.

Tiny shoulders

• Choose to "fill out" your shoulders with tops that have structure or volume: oversize knits or blazers, for instance.

• Opt for tops that reveal your cleavage while covering your shoulders, such as a heart-shaped neckline and puffy sleeves (but best to keep these for a night out rather than the daytime).

Dropped shoulders

• Envelope hemlines are a good choice as they embrace the natural shape of your shoulders.

Broad shoulders

• Go for anything that adds vertical lines to your silhouette. Your aim is to break up your upper body area into several thinner parts.
• Try V-neck tops and pendant necklaces.
• Layer! Fluid, thin and long layers without padding are perfect: lightweight blazers, silky kimonos, delicate knits…Avoid shorter layers that will just look boxy on you.
• Ensure that the shoulder–arm seam of your sleeves sits right at the edge of your shoulders.
• Avoid envelope-style hemlines, racerback, strapless or off-the-shoulder tops, which will make your shoulders look broader.

Arms

Your arms add a lot of character to your silhouette, so choose the shapes that will suit them best.

Super-thin arms

- Opt for sleeves that have some structure and/or are made with a stiff and/or thick fabric.
- Puffy sleeves, velvet shirts/jackets, cotton shirts or wool blazers are some of the tops that would be flattering on you.

Chubby arms

- Choose shapes that fit loosely around your shoulders and arms. It should never look as though your arm is being "strangled" by the sleeve and the fabric should not be stretched.
- With short sleeves, I recommend you cover the tops of your arms with diagonally-cut, flowy sleeves.
- With long sleeves, go for width, such as on kimonos.
- Avoid tops with thin straps. The wider the straps, the thinner your arms will appear.

Strong arms with broad shoulders

When you wear sleeveless tops, enhance your muscular frame and make your arms appear smaller with tops that stop at the edge of your shoulders and not before.

Breasts

Aaaah, breasts, something male designers often forget about, duh. Therefore, those of us with medium or small boobs have it easier when it comes to picking clothes. But don't worry, with the following tips, there is hope for all, *les filles*.

Small breasts

…on a petite frame
- You can add "body" to your upper torso with voluminous fabrics, such as angora wool or oversize knits, or detailing such as ruffles and knots.
- Wear some structured layers such as a blazer or a jean jacket.
- Ornament your chest with jewels: embellished necklines, a necklace…
- For a sexy look, embrace your delicate figure with plunging décolletages or very thin, tight or loose tops worn without a bra.

…on a grande frame
- Go for low-cut V-neck tops in fluid fabrics.
- For something dressier, try empire waistlines.

Large breasts

- Ensure that your jacket doesn't vanish at the sides when undone or gape open at the top when done up.
- Check that your shirt buttons do not pull across your breasts and that the fabric doesn't flatten your breasts out. Go for shirt styles in fluid fabrics and wear them open at the neck with the sleeves rolled up, to lighten the look.
- Avoid detailing on top: no fluffy material, ruffles, adornments…
- Avoid super-tight tops with crew necks or high necklines.
- Low necklines are flattering but much more chic when they don't reach the cleavage line.
- Avoid tight, high-waisted bottoms that make your breasts pop, "Jessica Rabbit style".
- Wear small necklaces that sit on your chest, not your breasts.

…and a flat belly
- To define your figure and prevent the "tent" effect, tuck or half-tuck your top into your low-waisted bottoms.

…and a defined waist
- Whether you are petite or chubby, tops or dresses with a defined waist (belted, cinched, knotted…) will enhance your hourglass figure.

…and a rounded belly
- Opt for fluid tops with low necklines that are neither tight nor wide and stop level with your hips. You could layer these with blazers or cardigans.

195

Waist

Since men do not have one, this feature is considered to be very womanly. However, that doesn't mean you have to have a defined waist in order to look feminine.

Straight

I am referring to those of you who have an androgynous, thin body without a defined waist.

- Most tops – whether straight, loose or with a structure – will suit you. But avoid all bodycon outfits that will draw attention to the absence of a waist, such as high-waisted jeans with tight tops.

- Create the illusion of a waist by belting loose tops and dresses: an oversize shirt with a belt, for instance, or a loose T-shirt with a high-waisted skater skirt. Make sure the belted area is significantly smaller than the areas above and below, *et voilà*.

Thick

- Choose straight tops and dresses that fit fairly close to your body but are neither tight nor hugging your midsection (avoid loose, thin T-shirts, for instance).
- Layering will make your midsection appear slimmer.
- Trying to give the illusion of a waist by wearing a belt, wrap dress or trench coat doesn't work, as it will set the focus on the circumference of your midsection, which is not the aim.
- If you have medium-sized breasts and a narrow ribcage, you could try empire waistlines.

Defined

You have THE hourglass figure that everyone has been crazy about since… prehistory. Size doesn't matter, only proportions do.

- Of course, you can take advantage of this asset and wear belted, cinched and bodycon tops and dresses… But you don't always have to.

Below the Waist

Hips

They don't lie: and if you have them, you're probably a woman. Hips are one of a few features that only women own, which is why it is considered attractive to emphasize them. But, again, a lack of hips can also be the starting point of equally creative and feminine styles.

Straight

Hips only look straight in comparison to the waist. So, straight hips always come without a defined waistline, whether your body is thin or thick overall.

• Go for straight or wide tops with straight bottoms. For example, fluid, loose or stiff tops with skinny, straight or cigarette trousers.

• Tight or bodycon skirts also look very good on you. What matters is that the bottom half is tight on the hips.

• Add volume around your hips with long layers, such as blazers, kimonos or cardigans.

• If you have a slender body, create the illusion of an hourglass figure with bottoms that add volume at the sides. Try trapeze skirts, skater skirts, skirts with pockets and carrot trousers.

• Embrace a boyish style with low-waisted boyfriend jeans.

Wide

Your ideal hourglass figure looks spectacular with bodycon, belted or cinched shapes but that's not to say you can't relax your look.

• Go for silhouettes that enhance the waist and the hips, such as A-line skirts, skater skirts and tight, high-waisted skirts or trousers.

• On days when you would like your figure to look less va-va-voom, give the illusion of narrower hips with fluid or straight tops that stop at the widest point of the hips: this will lessen the contrast between your waist and hips.

• Pair fluid or straight tops with skinny jeans, straight trousers and straight stiff or fluid skirts.

• To make your hips appear thinner, balance them with flared bottoms. My favourites are flares or bell-bottom trousers that are fitted at the top before getting wider.

Booty

I chose to consider the booty separately from the hips because the booty is visible from the side and back whereas hips are visible from the front and back. It is possible to have no hips and a rounded booty or vice versa.

Regular or flat booty

- If you look straight when viewed from the side, try to wear longer tops and layers. Or anything where the booty is "invisible", such as A-line, straight or flowy dresses.
- You could also go for dresses and skirts with pleats, ruffles and anything that adds volume.
- If you would like to make your booty look rounder, try "shaping" jeans with extra contouring.

Bouncy booty

- Any trousers or skirt that are both high-waisted and tight will underline your assets.
- Belted, cinched, structured or bodycon dresses will look flattering on you.
- If you would like your curves to be less visible, opt for fluid bottoms and longer tops.
- A-line, straight and long, flowy dresses will also make your booty disappear.
- You may have problems with jeans and trousers being too wide at your lower back. Look for brands that have styles designed for "curvy" shapes. Otherwise, have your jeans altered to fit you.

Legs

The days when Coco Chanel made women knee-conscious – considering them so ugly that she advised women to always cover them – have long gone. Nowadays at the house of Chanel, King Karl creates tweed mini skirts. Whether you feel like displaying your knees or not, here's how to get your legs looking fabulous.

Short legs

- To make the best of your legs, go short. Mini skirts and shorts are for you.
- If you do not feel comfortable with your skin on show, wear opaque or semi-opaque tights (pantyhose).
- Opt for skinny jeans that define the shape of your legs, if they are curvy; if they are super-thin, however, straight trousers are preferable.
- Want to lengthen your silhouette? Opt for shoes the colour of your bare legs, or wear dark shoes with matching tights (pantyhose). If wearing flat shoes, choose ones that have thick soles and that sit below the ankle.
- Try flared jeans with platform shoes, to create the illusion of longer legs.
- If your legs are shorter than your torso, balance your proportions with short tops and high-waisted trousers.
- If you have a chubby midsection, go for fluid tops that stop just below the belly.

Long legs

- Lucky you, all trouser and skirt lengths look wonderful on you; you can easily sport midi-length and floor-length dresses and skirts.
- If you are tall with long legs, mini skirts and shorts can appear very sexy (because there is so much skin on show). For a more relaxed look, balance them with flats.
- If your legs are long in comparison to your torso, choose tops that reach at least to the hips.

Thick legs

- Stay away from trousers or skirts that have side pockets and from trousers that have a front pleat (unless the pleat has been sewn in place and will not flatten out on wearing).
- To lessen the contrast between your calves and your feet, choose wide or platform heels and thick-soled flats.
- When wearing a midi-length skirt, always add some heels to ensure your silhouette does not look stubby.

Super-thin legs

• Choose tiny or
delicate heels.
• If you wear trousers,
add some volume to
them with thick fabrics.

203

Shades for Your Skin Tone

Back in the Eighties, there was a huge trend for "having your colours done". According to the shade of your skin and its undertone, in combination with your hair colour, a specialist would determine what "season" you were and then give you a list of the colours you should wear. This may sound like an excellent guideline but it generated anxiety when shopping because the colours that were trending often did not include the ones that had been recommended to you. I had clients who came to me, a bit lost, telling me that the limited range of shades in their palettes was difficult to source and sometimes felt quite old-fashioned.

Even if I think that some colours really DO enhance the beauty of one's complexion, any recommendations shouldn't be too directive or too limiting. And they only apply to the colours next to your face. You can wear whatever colour you fancy on your shoes. You can also balance the colour that doesn't flatter you with one that does. For instance, if beige washes you out, you could still wear it and look good if you compensate with a colour that complements you. So when you wear a beige trench coat, add a coral scarf or a coral lipstick.

The colour insights I will give you on the following pages are deliberately quite vague and the shades I name are merely suggestions of what *could* look good on you. Besides, to "dress like a Parisian", the basis of an outfit mainly relies on neutrals with a hint of colour, no matter what the colour of your skin is. If you choose the perfect shade for you, that's even better.

Fair skin

Here I mean pale white skin with rosy cheeks and icy blue veins on the wrist. I often meet clients with such complexions who wear mostly black, giving themselves a severe look. They stay away from paler shades in the belief that they will make them look washed-out, when in fact quite the opposite happens.

Blonde

- Pale grey, beige and white are your perfect neutrals. Avoid cream colours that will wash you out.
- Soft shades such as dusty pastels and muted tones will underline your porcelain complexion.
- Worried about looking dull? Incorporate soft shine, such as gold, rose gold and silver, or a pop of a more pigmented colour. Chartreuse yellow, Barbie pink and coral are all excellent accents, for instance. Khaki is also a good complement to the white, beige and rosy tones of this palette.
- Then add some mascara and a hint of rosewood or coral blush and/or lipstick to freshen up your face.
- A warm classic brown and caramel palette is a classy option for elegant outfits. You could finish these bourgeois looks with burgundy lipstick.
- For dressier styles, navy blue is the perfect alternative to black. In the same classic vibe, you could also try forest green or burgundy.
- When you want to look spectacular, you could pick a black dress. Wear it with a no-makeup look for an edgy style, or with either eye makeup or red lips for a glamorous result.

Brunette

- White, beige and black are your perfect neutrals.
- Try sugary pastels, such as mint green, baby blue, milky pink or pale yellow, or bold colours if you are looking for a witty style.
- Dark shades, such as black and gold, will underline your gothic beauty. Go for deep purple, burgundy or forest green.
- Opt for red lips for a bold style or coral for a fresh effect.

Redhead

- White, beige, navy blue, grey and black are your perfect neutrals.
- To make your hair look even more magnificent, contrast it with dark green or blue clothes.
- If you want to surprise, dare to wear warm, bold shades, such as red, pink, yellow, purple or even lilac.
- Silver, gold and coloured metallics are brightening options.

Medium skin

By medium skin, I mean pale women who get a light tan in summer. Whatever your hair tone, most colours suit you.
- Beige, grey, white, cream, navy blue and black are your perfect neutrals, and brown, caramel, taupe and almost-neutral shades will warm up your complexion.
- Accent with a lipstick in coral, poppy, bright or deep red, and accessories in any bright shade.
- A statement piece in red or any other warm colour is a wise choice, and muted shades of blue and green will create a pretty contrast with your skin.
- Choose pinks that have yellow undertones, and stay away from icy colours, such as mint green or sapphire.
- Favour gold, rose gold or copper jewellery.

Tan skin

Gals with tan skin include those with brunette hair in shades ranging from chestnut brown to super-dark and with Indian, Latino, Chinese or Afro-Caucasian origins. What differs is the undertone in their skin.

Olive complexion
- Your perfect neutrals are white, cream, grey, navy blue and black. Avoid beiges that are too similar to your complexion.
- White really brightens your face; pair it with natural leather, gold or silver jewellery.
- As for statement colours or accents, go for jewel shades such as emerald, sapphire, pink or purple amethyst. Sunshine yellow and neon colours are also options.

Golden complexion
- Your perfect neutrals are white, cream, sand and black.
- White is also perfect to brighten up your skin. You could mix it with dusty colours in pinkish tones, earthy khaki and gold accents.
- Warm colours suit you perfectly. If you want to go bold, try cherry red, dark apricot or mushy green.
- For classic dark shades, try midnight blue or black.

Dark skin
- If you have a very deep skin tone, aim to wear light shades and saturated colours in order to create a contrast.
- Your perfect neutrals are white, cream, beige and black. Accent them with gold and bright red or blue to create elegant, easy-to-wear everyday outfits.
- When you want to go bold, opt for highly saturated colours, such as vibrant blue, sunny yellow or cherry red.
- Whitened cold shades, such as lavender blue or banana yellow, also work for you.

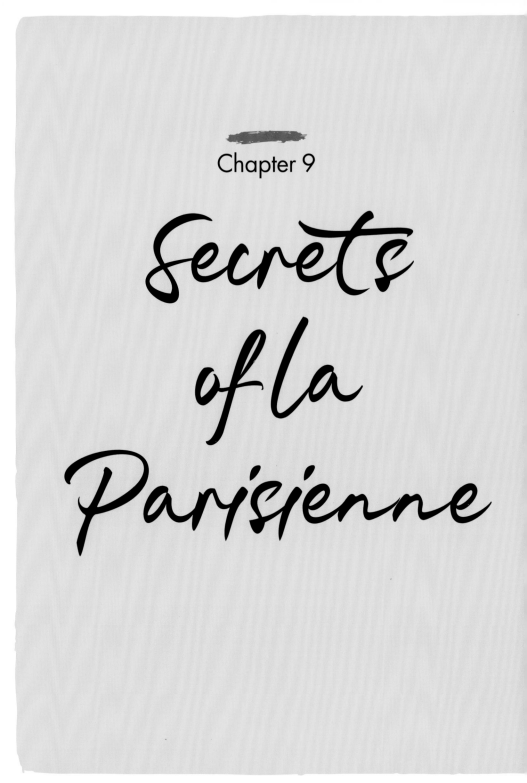

Chapter 9

Secrets of la Parisienne

The Art of Parisian Style

Lots of French dresses have pockets, which is apparently quite unusual in other countries, resulting in a mix of elegance and nonchalance that is so emblematic of Parisian style. There is more to it than clothing; it's an attitude, a way of behaving, a whole art of styling and buying. That's the unique take *les Parisiennes* have on sexiness. Their is a mixture of classicism and freedom in all things, the way they live in their clothes and their independent thinking about to trends that leads them to manage their purchases and closets in a responsible way (before it was cool).

To dress like *les Parisiennes*, you need to understand their approach to clothes: how they purchase them, how they store them, how they live with them and how, sometimes, they get rid of them.

In this chapter I am going to share the insights of professionals in the worlds of hair, beauty and underwear; the Parisian's take on sexiness; how to tell good clothes from bad; how to organize your closet and style what's in it.

"To dress like les Parisiennes, you need to understand their approach to clothes"

Be Subtly Sexy

One of the ingredients of the French *"je ne sais quoi"* is sexiness. Not that of a woman who conforms to society standards but of a woman who "owns" her clothes. The first person she is trying to please is herself, but that's not to say she doesn't take others into consideration. She may dress to impress for a work event, put together a polished look for meeting her conservative in-laws or pull out all the stops to seduce a hot date.

For this purpose, you should know what clothes look appealing on your own body, what has an effect on others (or on a specific person, but, hey, I don't know your *chéri*) and also some easy triggers that make an outfit sensual – in the French way, of course.

For us, being sexy is about being suggestive, so we like to play "conceal and reveal" with our clothes. An oversize sweater with the neckline slipping to expose a shoulder, a delicate ankle between trouser and shoe… In fact, the more you cover up, the more an exposed body part will stand out. Your ankle will go unnoticed in a super-tight, super-short minidress, but it will be the centre of attention in cropped trousers.

Top five sexy elements

1. Delicate fabrics

Silk, cashmere and leather are all very sensual fabrics. The silk glides over your body, moving like fluid water around you when you walk. The cashmere caresses your skin, making your outfit feel as soft as you do. Thin leather becomes your second skin – removing leather gloves can be mesmerizing.

2. Raw fabrics

I am a fan of the contrast between a rough material, such as thick jeans, vintage leather or imperfect fabrics, and a soft skin.

3. See-through fabrics

Either a little or very transparent; use them to play with mystery and even to reveal the silhouette of your underwear.

4. Dressing like a boy

This is something that is often considered very erotic. Think Marlene Dietrich's style, Yves Saint Laurent's iconic Le Smoking suit and (smokin' hot) Charlotte Rampling undressed in *The Night Porter* (1974). Or, simply, men loving it when their girlfriend borrows their clothes.

5. Dressing like a femme fatale

Her characteristic would be to act and dress in a way that is considered in our culture to be extremely womanly: a grown-up, strong woman who knows what she wants and is confident in her seductive power. The literal translation of *"fatale"* is "deadly".

Unexpected body parts to highlight

The ear

Wear an ear cuff or an earring on one side only. Tie your hair to the side, like Lauren Bacall or Rihanna.

The collarbone

Undo an extra button on your shirt or add a delicate gold chain.

"La nuque" (the nape of your neck)

Short hair cut? You're already there. Otherwise, tie your hair up loosely and let a few strands fall loose.

Back and shoulders

Open-back tops are obviously a sexy option. For more subtlety, wear a V-neck cashmere – maybe it'll slip off your shoulder revealing your bra strap…It's OK as long as it is a delicate one.

Cut-out dresses

Dare to wear a dress with cut-outs that expose skin in unexpected places.

Wrists and ankles

Cropped trousers and shorter sleeves are your allies. Decorate wrists with delicate or chunky jewellery that will draw attention to the area as you move.

A hint of thigh

The part of the thigh that sits exposed above over-the-knee socks or boots is an extremely erotized body part. The Japanese call it *"Zettai Ryōiki"*. To bare without going tacky, wear decent clothes up top. A chunky sweater with over-the-knee boots is perfect, for instance. You could also try tights (pantyhose) that look like suspenders with a very discreet outfit.

Beauty *au Naturel*

Plenty of style icons are famous for not wearing a hint of mascara. *Especially* in the fashion world, where people are more free about the way they dress. Parisian designer Isabel Marant has been going barefaced with her grey hair tied into a high bun for years. And lots of people are prone to wearing makeup or not depending on the day and their mood, which means they do not consider makeup as mandatory. And why should they? Our male counterparts are not expected to wear it. So why should we feel obliged to spend 20 minutes applying it every morning?

Don't get me wrong, I love using makeup as a tool to improve a style, but it shouldn't become a constraint, something that you *have* to apply every morning. Just as women shouldn't be forced to wear heels to conform to social conventions, makeup should merely be an option.

When French women wear makeup, they do it in order to enhance their beauty or to play with it but not to design themselves a new face. Therefore, heavy makeup trends, such as contouring, fake eyelashes or bold brows, never encounter the widespread success here that they do in other countries.

I had a talk with Sarina Lavagne d'Ortigue, founder of Prescription Lab, a high-quality beauty box and cosmetics brand, about what *les Parisiennes* use on their faces in the morning.

What would be a *Parisienne's* beauty routine?
What matters most is beautiful skin. French women use scrub, moisturizer and masks with consistency. Then they apply makeup to enhance their beauty. In terms of colours, they prefer natural shades, such as soft rose or brown for daytime, and mascara to make the eyes pop. If they want a *femme fatale* look, all they need is a bright red lipstick.

La Parisienne has fun with makeup, which she considers a way to express her personality. She'll use it to underline her personal features rather than trying to look like a star or an influencer. A blonde with thick brows may accentuate them; a redhead with freckles won't try to conceal them.

Is "no makeup" a real thing?
Well, when you are Isabel Marant you can make a fashion statement out of it, but for most women it is important to wear at least a light base in order not to look unkempt.

Hair *au Naturel*

Oh là là! Les cheveux à la Parisienne…How do we get this natural wave, this brunette shade, this *négligé* (scruffy and undone) attitude? I'll tell you a secret. Effortless is no myth. French girls are not very good at managing their hair themselves. They will condition it and (sometimes) blow-dry it but that's about it. Occasionally they'll go for braids, a messy bun or a ponytail. But this "French girl hair fantasy" is limited to bohemian style. Except maybe in the west of Paris, where blonde hair is more popular and blow-drying is better mastered.

I asked Vinz, creative director of luxury haircare brand Leonor Greyl, for his insights into the hairstyles of Parisian beauties.

How would you define Parisian hairstyle?
I would say it is rock and roll. A typical Parisian hairstyle would be the "done then undone blow-dry". *Parisiennes* are looking for quick and effective; they don't want to spend too much time on it. And *naturel*. When French actresses come to me to have their hair styled, they always say *"pas trop"*, which means "not too much". They do not want their hair to look overprocessed so they stay away from ironed-sleek or curled styles. When you are a twenty-something, you do little or nothing. Then the more you age, the more polished your hair gets, but you never end up with something too rigid.

Can you tell me how the blow-dry of *"les blondes of the seizième arrondissement"* is different from the American version?
It is less high. The hairdresser lifts the roots with the hairdryer and brushes. This is called *"brushing à la Carita"*, from the name of the salon that invented it. The ultimate reference is Catherine Deneuve. Those ladies go to their hairdresser every two days

to have their styling done. That's actually what hairdressers were for before Vidal Sassoon invented haircuts.

So what about Parisian haircuts?
Hair-wise, the Parisian girl prefers to blend in. (Probably because she doesn't want her hair to get all the attention by choosing something eccentric). If she *does* want to make a statement, she'll just go for a fringe or a bob.

Are extensions popular?
As long as they look natural. *Parisiennes* also use additional clip-in hairpieces to add volume to thin hair: to make a topknot look more voluminous or a long bob fuller, for instance.

And hair colour?
You keep it natural and just enhance your natural beauty with highlights or a slightly darker shade. If you've got white hair, you'll ask for your natural colour.

And what about women who decide to keep their white hair, like the influential journalist Sophie Fontanel, who just published a book about her colour transitioning?
Being out with grey or white hair proves a strong character and can be very trendy. With the right outfit, this is definitely rock. And on an elderly woman with a perfect blow-dry, it becomes super-chic. You just have to maintain it well with conditioner and shampoo that contain blue in order to avoid yellow highlights.

What would be a typical "evening" hairstyle?
Something easy to master like a "*chignon banane*" (a "French pleat". Of course).

Style Your Clothes on You

In French, we say "*habiter un vêtement*". Which translates as "live in a garment" or "make the garment live". A piece of clothing on a hanger is lifeless, which is why collections are presented on moving models rather than just in showrooms. And since each woman is different, you cannot just put the clothes on her and go. That's why there are stylists backstage, who arrange the clothes on the models, adjusting folds, adding a belt here, ripping a neckline more open there and even performing last-minute tailoring adjustments.

When you purchase a garment, be like a stylist and do the same…Make alterations if necessary and then arrange it with other pieces to compose an interesting outfit. The glory of some garments is that you can style them a million (well, OK, three or four) different ways.

Have your clothes altered

Of course it is best to buy clothes that suit you to perfection already. But since ready-to-wear, as its name implies, is "ready", it can't be for everyone, and alterations may have to be done. Do not turn your back on a piece of clothing that is almost perfect just because it needs a minor modification, such as a strap shortened or a waistline tightened.

Ask the salesperson or, even better, the store's tailor (department stores always hire one) whether or not the alteration is possible and if the cost of the service is worth it before you purchase.

Please do not feel that you are a "bad size" because clothes always need to be altered to fit you. It is impossible that all women on Earth would fit the standard sizes, isn't it? My clients often complain that they are midgets because trousers are always far too long. Well, manufacturers do this "in case" there are some very tall and thin women wanting to purchase the same size as you. Do not feel bad; in my experience, only women taller than 1.8m (6ft) get not to pay tailoring fees.

Do not postpone the alteration. Otherwise, your garment will lie, sad and abandoned, in your closet forever, its delightful taste being appreciated only by moths (what a tragic fate).

Style your clothes…throughout the day

Observe a stylish woman putting a piece of clothing on. She will pull one side, flatten the folds, appreciate the effect, open one more button, roll the sleeves and so on.

Copy her and arrange your clothes until they are well positioned. I have already shared some little tricks on how to roll up a sleeve and tie a scarf (*see* pages 111 and 152–3), but do you know the trick for tucking a top into a high-waisted skirt? Push the top beneath the waistband of your skirt, then lift up your skirt and pull the top down from underneath, smoothing the fabric so that it sits flat beneath your skirt (hope no one enters the room at this stage). If your top is fluid, gently pull it very slightly up again so that it doesn't appear "stuck".

Throughout the day you will move, use the bathroom, dance, kiss, LIVE…and your clothes will not stay where they should. Style them again. It may sound demanding but the stylish girls do not even THINK about it. It's as simple as reapplying lipstick.

Customize your clothes

Only basics, inherited pieces and clothes from second-hand and thrift stores are usually worth being customized. Yes, to cropping a pair of jeans with scissors. Yes, to embroidering the name of your Persian cat on your T-shirt. Yes, to dyeing those white jeans a baby pink because, why not? Yes, to adding patches to this cool jean jacket. Yes, to making a top out of that vintage silk scarf (congrats, you are quite gifted with your hands). And yes, to sewing sequins wherever it pleases you.

But don't buy more sophisticated (and expensive) clothes with the idea that you'll customize them, even if it is to remove the annoying knot that has been put on a shoulder or to change the colour by dyeing it. Usually, they will have been designed with care and will be really tricky to alter.

Freedom Lingerie

Did you know the French invented knickers and nylon tights (pantyhose) – two innovations that aimed to free women from underwear constraints? The former was created in 1918 by a brand named Petit Bateau; the latter developed following the invention of nylon by chemist Éleuthère Irénée du Pont de Nemours in 1938.

Since the seventeenth century, our libertine traditions had developed a taste for all things delicate and suggestive, with lace, ribbons and silk being popular underwear staples. Both our bodies and mindsets are free when it comes to lingerie. Which is probably why, in 2016, the century-old French underwear brand Etam named its big catwalk show "French Liberté".

I asked Anne-Sophie Goblet, a brand and trends consultant specializing in lingerie, what the *Parisiennes* were wearing underneath.

Describe Parisian lingerie in two words
Effortlessly sexy. Parisian eroticism is about suggestion more than about being sculptural. The sexiness is never too obvious.

What are the popular bra shapes?
Cup bras and balconette bras are two of the most popular shapes. Parisians look for comfort and lightness first. They are not much into heavily padded or push-up styles. More and more new brands are also creating very thin and transparent underwear that is close to the skin. For instance, the tagline of the young brand Ysé, which claims to do padding-free lingerie to embrace a woman's body, is "You are naturally perfect". There is even a revival of Seventies feminism, with young women no longer wearing bras. In France, it's not a problem to see the shape of a nipple. Those "free" bras are a way to empower yourself.

What is the style of Parisian lingerie?
Well, effortlessly sexy, but also fun and fashionable. You can play with your underwear as you would with any other fashion items. Therefore, bras have various styles, from playful sexiness, *à la Brigitte Bardot*, to something ultra-sophisticated. When dressed, you can reveal a bit of your underwear in your outfits: a strap, a bodysuit, a camisole…

Layer Like a Pro

We use the idiom "dressing like *un oignon*" to say that we layer clothes in order to stay warm. An onion doesn't sound like a very glamorous style routine, does it? But, besides looking super-stylish, layering is for more than just warmth; it is a great way to adapt to every moment of the day and can help you use your thin clothes, such as dresses and blouses, in colder weather. Let me share my tips on how to become a stylish onion. (As your thermal underwear is none of my business, I will only talk about the outer layers that are visible.)

Shapes

When worn open, waistcoats, blazers and cardigans should fall straight and vertically without creating a triangle shape or hiding under the armpits. If you find a fabric heavy enough, you'll avoid this problem.

Pay attention to hemlines and necklines. Do not ruin your V-neck with a round neckline showing underneath. If you feel your V is too deep, choose a bustier (or a lookalike). The same goes for square-looking Chanel-like jackets that demand low necklines.

Victorian or turtleneck collars are a great way to spice up your crew-neck sweaters and shirts while also warming them up.

Style tip

There are two kinds of layering:
- Vertical layering – when opened layers create vertical lines.
- Horizontal layering – when the top layers are shorter than the one(s) underneath.

Think of layering over a long shirt, where the collar, sleeves and hem will all show, to punctuate outfits.

Allowing the bottom of a pale T-shirt to show between a dark sweater and trousers adds definition and structures the silhouette.

Fabrics

Wear the thickest and stiffest piece of clothing on top, otherwise you will look like a poorly stuffed teddy bear.

The fabrics should look different from each other. A jersey T-shirt over a jersey T-shirt will look quite geeky and your outfit will lack shape. (OK, the twinset isn't *that* bad, but it's a tad conservative, isn't it?) Yet you could layer similar fabrics. For instance, a thin jean shirt under a stiff jean jacket, or a fine, tight knit under a loose, oversize knit.

Layer see-through fabrics for creative and subtle outfits: an open-weave knit over a camisole or a transparent turtleneck top under a crew-neck sweater, for example.

Layering loose and oversize with structured and stiff has a super-stylish effect: try a fitted biker jacket over a floppy T-shirt or big knit.

Lengths

When you do vertical layering, you could go classic with the top layers, making them longer than the underneath layers. For instance, a T-shirt and a jean shirt underneath a boyish blazer. But you could also combine it with horizontal layering and use short layers on top. For instance, an oversize cashmere V-neck topped with a short, stiff jean jacket.

When you do horizontal layering, don't fear unusual mixes. Why not top a long, stiff cotton shirt with a cropped sweater? Or wear long sleeves under a sleeveless top. Or a T-shirt under a bustier.

How many layers?

I recommend two or three, with four being the maximum (for style ninjas only).
• First layer (the thinnest): dress, T-shirt, shirt, thin knit, sweater
• Second layer: open shirt, cardigan, knits, jean jacket
• Third layer: jean jacket, cardigan
• Fourth layer: coat

Get Creative

No matter what clothes you wear, no matter how you mix them, you can feel that you always look the same while your colleague seems to be reinventing her look every day. Instead of just admiring her, try to learn lessons from her. You could try to break down her outfits in order to get inspiration. Wondering why this grey office skirt looks great on her? Observe how she positions it, what shoes she pairs it with and whether she did or didn't tuck her top into it. When you've identified what you like, find a way to adapt it on yourself. In the end, observation and analysis, paired with realism, are the best ways to get fashionably creative.

Be realistic

Creativity is often boosted by constraints. In fashion, your constraints could be that you are invited to a green-themed wedding in the woods. Which implies that you have to find some green-coloured clothes, a top layer because the woods may be cold at night-time and shoes that you can walk in on muddy grass…Which can totally sound like a pain but is actually the best way to get out of your comfort zone. Let's be honest, you would never have worn green if it was up to you and it looks amazing.

Inspiration is all around

Observing how fashion is done by others is the best way to train your eye and get inspired. Look around, inspiration can come from anywhere.

- The lady in the street who is balancing her cropped trousers with high-heeled ankle boots.
- The TV ad, in which the redhead (just like you) wears a yellow dress and the colour suits her perfectly.
- The catwalk footage, where the models are wearing suits with sneakers.
- The magazine photos, where the stylist has mixed fishnets with corduroy trousers.
- And even pictures of the house, where the leather sofas match the cream knitted cushions so well.
- From the rhubarb stalks, in which green and pink look so harmonious together.
- Educate yourself about fashion; the more trained your eye, the better you'll get. Read books about fashion history and designers, buy magazines, look at fashion blogs and observe the styles of the ladies around you.

Beauty in the Detail

Do you have some pieces in your wardrobe that are really complicated to combine with others? There are two explanations for this:
1. They are interesting, stylish pieces, aka statement pieces, that are self-sufficient. You just need to combine them with basics to create amazing outfits.
2. They contain superfluous details.

Superfluous details

Women often choose this kind of clothing when they do not dare go for the big thing but have a desire to spice up their style. However, now you've almost finished this book, you know that all you need to be stylish is a lot of basics along with a few statement pieces and accessories.

A piece of clothing with superfluous details contains tiny little elements that aren't noticeable enough to improve your style but that will remind you of their existence each time you try to match them. You'll mostly find them in fast fashion on otherwise random basic clothes. Just as if the details have been added to make the piece of clothing interesting. Which they won't. With high-end or luxury clothes, the details are likely to be so skilfully executed that they will actually enhance the beauty of the piece.

Some superfluous details to avoid

- Crystal-patched elbows on a knit: won't make your elbows glam or funky… but will make this little cardigan super-difficult to pair.
- Poor-quality, tiny polyester fringes: won't give any "Western vibes" to your outfit. Better opt for longer suede ones.
- Sewn bows: will look flat, creased and miserable quickly. There are tons of better options to make your top look girly.
- Spike-adorned T-shirts: will alter quickly and are tricky to match: why not wear costume jewellery instead?

Style tips

- Replace ready-made adornments with DIY styling. Instead of buying a pair of jeans with just a few crystal embellishments, wear crystal bracelets. You'll get the glam when you want it and will be able to use the jeans as part of more casual outfits, without worrying about the crystals not matching.
- When buying a piece that is not a basic, ask yourself the following question: if I wear this piece with plain jeans or a plain T-shirt, will I look stylish or elegant? If the answer is no, then pass.

Style-enhancing details

These are difficult to differentiate from the superfluous details. Yet these actually add something to the garment (*see* picture below), including details that you notice enough for the garment to qualify as "a stylish piece", enhancing the overall fabric while remaining understated enough to make it easy to match. Such details usually imply good-quality fabric and design.

Bold details

These are the details that give enough attitude to a garment to make it more than just a basic. Such as:
- the serrated shape of your collar
- the pussy bow around your neck
- the heavily padded shoulders of your top
- the large buttons down your dress
- the flounces around your skirt

Discreet details

These are the details that won't be noticed immediately but will give your style an overall refinement that will be appreciated. Such as:
- your quality mother-of-pearl buttons
- the single pocket of your jeans
- the belt around your waist
- the colour of the soles of your shoes

Optimize Your Closet

Each morning, the same stressful routine: you open your closet and nothing feels appealing…there is just too much of it. Your dozens of boring grey staples, dresses from your pin-up era next to your new-you edgy tops. Jeans in doubtful colours from the Noughties. There's even something with shoulder pads from the Eighties that your mum gave you there…Or, you just run into…a quite empty closet. Which is as annoying as looking into an empty fridge each morning.

I have encountered both these closets at my clients' homes; the first one being by far the most common in our consumerist society. In both situations, you need some closet optimization. Here is the method I use with my clients.

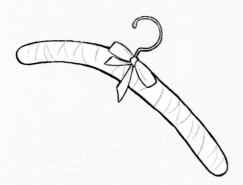

1. Have a sort out

Separate your clothes and accessories (shoes, jewellery, coats, everything you wear) and sort them into three piles:
- Clothes you wear daily
- Clothes you like but do not wear
- Clothes you do not like

Then it's time to analyse. This process can be undertaken by yourself, after having read this book, or with an honest and (even better) stylish friend or a personal stylist.

Clothes you wear daily
In this pile, my clients often put the basics, the clothes that fit them best and easy-to-match statement pieces.

Ask yourself the following questions:
- Why do you wear these clothes so often?
- What do you like about them?
- Are they easy to style?
- Do you flatter your silhouette or complexion? Why and how?

Then examine them with care. Sometimes you may have worn an item so often that you do not notice it has changed. Be honest here. Has this knit pilled? Is this black top washed out? Can you get those yellow stains under the armpits white again? Is the alteration worth it? If the answer is no, get rid of it.

Clothes you like but do not wear
When my clients show me this pile, I often find a mix of pieces that are not flattering, pieces with superfluous details, pieces that do not match their style family (such as boho clothes in an otherwise classic wardrobe) and sometimes statement pieces – gems that are only here because they are difficult to style but have great unexploited potential.

Ask yourself the following questions:
• Why don't you wear these clothes?
• Do they flatter you? If not, why not?
• Are they difficult to match?
• Are they comfortable?
• Do you think they are your style?

Clothes you do not like

Most of my clients are quite aware of what looks really bad on them, and I rarely find any good things in this pile...but it may happen that I find a little hidden treasure. Get a stylist or a friend who is able to see the potential to check these out with you.

If you are by yourself, just get rid of them. There is no point in keeping pieces you do not like in your wardrobe and it is unlikely you'll get rid of anything amazing.

2. Get organized

Clothes

First, seperate items according to season (winter/summer) and put your out-of-season belongings away and out of sight. Then separate the clothes that are meant to be hung from the ones that have to be folded. Always separate the sport and night clothes from the rest, too.

Now you can begin to sort your clothes into categories. If you do not have a lot of clothes and/or you have a tiny closet, sorting tops, sweaters, layers, bottoms and dresses into piles is sufficient. If you have more clothes, create subcategories. Within the tops, separate casual from dressy and basic from statement. It is always handy to have a pile of basic tops you can dig into when searching for a layering base.

You can then proceed to organize your other items in the same way.

Jewellery

Get yourself a proper jewellery box so you can see everything you own. Hanging necklaces on the wall and earrings on a dedicated hanger is also a great way to keep everything on view.

Other accessories

Store each category in a single place. Gather the bags together, find a display rack for the shoes, hang the scarves next to each other, do the same for the belts, find a box for the gloves, one for socks... If accessories can be found in several places all around the house, chances are you will forget about the existence of some.

3. Throw, sell, donate?

Throwing

A big no; definitely not responsible Earth-conscious behaviour.

Selling

The process of selling second-hand clothes is often quite complicated. I recommend you sell only valuable designer clothes that are in perfect shape. Otherwise, it's often just an excuse to keep your clothing in the limbo of indecision.

Donating

This is the option I recommend because it is both quick and helpful to charities.

"Just in case"

One dirty T-shirt is enough "just in case" you will be painting your walls. You do not need seven of them, so donate or recycle the other six.

Thrifty Finds

Aaaah, thrift stores. Here in Paris, they are always a bit of a mess, with the clothes coming out from everywhere, the overcrowded hangers, the tiny aisle, the unidentified smell…I must say, the experience can be quite alarming for a rookie. That's why, if you are wandering without a purpose, you can quickly get dizzy and walk away without a thing (or with a grandma sweater you'll never wear).

When shopping in thrift stores, you have two options:
1. Meticulously check each item in the store, one by one. It may take you hours but you might find THE absolute gem.
2. Look for an item within a category of thrift store classics.

The army jacket

You can make this work with almost any casual outfit and use it to dress down sexy looks. To make it look "lighter", I suggest you roll up the sleeves and wear it open. It fits tall and curvy girls alike, but petite ladies should hunt for a small one or they'll look lost in it.

The jean jacket

Go for a super-tiny one, *à la* Hedi Slimane, or an oversize one, *à la Thelma et Louise*. Aim to find denim pieces made from a beautiful fabric; forget about anything stretchy or too monochrome.

The leather item

Thrift stores are full of leather: jackets, skirts, shorts, bags, boots…And this is good news because you can't get this expensive fabric much cheaper. Plus, the leather will have a cool, used style. But be cautious that the leather is not stained (such as by water) or scratched. A fitted piece will probably not suit you perfectly but you can always get it altered by your favourite tailor.

The little printed dress

Each decade created its batch of printed dresses. These are easy to wear, as you can just belt them to add some structure, or have them altered to fit.

The printed shirt

Aaaah, Eighties prints…if you were missing them, rejoice, they are waiting for you in the thrift stores. OK, some are kind of dubious, but that's the beauty of ugly. Worn with basics, they'll add a hint of hipster to your look. And if you are suspicious of them, choose prints from other decades.

Long or short jeans

Without a hint of elastane – so YES, they are hard to get into and YES, they are like a natural bypass when you sit for lunch, but they DO make the best bottom ever. Life choices. The most difficult part is to actually

find your perfect jeans match. It requires (a lot of) patience to try them all. If you feel like you want to be comfortable, you'll also find lots of low-waisted, cool boyfriend jeans options.

The glittery item

Glitter may fall but sequins do not get old. So if you spot a glittery thing in a thrift store that has not lost a single sequin, you can predict they'll hold on in there for the next decade. Jackets and little dresses are just perfect for partying like it is disco time. Or to mix into casual daytime outfits.

The scarf *"foulard"*

Hermès-style ones, soft ones from the Seventies and bandanas are to be found by the boxful. Dig around until you fall in love at first sight.

The printed T-shirt

Rather than buying a faux-old printed tee from a fast-fashion store, or an exorbitant one from Chanel, you'll get a real metal band or promotional tee for less than 10 euros. If it is oversize, improvise. Tuck it in your mini and cut or roll up the sleeves for a bad gal muscle top.

Forever- vs Fast-fashion

In the early twenty-first century, fashion collections escalated to four per year, capsules not included. The turnover of trends had never been so high. Brands were almost selling pieces with an expiry date. Even leather handbags, historically long-lasting items, became "it-bags": buy now before it's outdated. The feeling of rarity that used to be associated with high-end items diminished and consumers began to turn their backs on luxury brands. Nowadays, some brands take a different path, capitalizing on their know-how, the quality of their products and the stories behind their houses. Although some items aren't meant to last "forever", you shouldn't view accessories or clothing as disposable.

Choosing a forever bag

Aside from some eccentricities designed to please a small fringe of fashionistas, the majority of bag companies have returned to more timeless designs. When buying a bag, look for a timeless piece for your closet, as if you were buying it for a lifetime. Will you still like it two years from now? Is the shape comfortable enough for you to use? Does the bag feel high quality or it is too fragile?

Choosing forever clothing

Most pieces of clothing do not last as long as they used to and certainly not for a lifetime. Yet you can try to be reasonable when shopping for them. When investing in a piece of clothing, consider its lifespan (which I consider to be five years for a coat and three years for other clothes) and ask yourself if you will tire of it before it "dies". This should prevent you from clogging up your closet with short-term items that you will only ever wear once or twice.

Shopping fast-fashion

Having advocated the benefits of buying for a lifetime, I am aware that not everyone has the budget to invest in every item. On- and offline fast-fashion stores overflow with interesting items but be cautious: some may look more appealing in the picture or on the mannequin than on you. Be wise and learn how to tell the good from the bad.

How to avoid a fast-fashion *faux pas*

Check the fabric

The cheaper you go, the poorer the quality is likely to be. If you buy online, always check the zoom image and read the fabric composition. Beware bad synthetics that can appear shiny – not in a good way – and super-lightweight fabrics (used because they are cheaper to produce and transport) that can appear see-through. Do not go cheap on items that require a quality fabric to look good, such as coats and knits. Cheaper shoes and scarves are also risky bets. Nothing will make your outfit go from chic to cheap faster than a poor-quality scarf.

Check the finish

Copying couture is not always successful. It can work well when it is just about a pattern, a cool shape or a new texture, but some more sophisticated finishes are simply harder to reproduce. Always check the quality of the stitching and that it is not already falling apart.

Go basic

Complete your outfits with cheap basics. You can't go wrong with T-shirts, shirts or jeans.

Avoid superfluous details

As we saw on page 226, details do not do well when cheaply executed.

Dare to be fashionable

Instead of investing in a gold metallic cropped top or pleated mini skirt, buy them for a lower price. The shine will hide the flaws and make them look more expensive.

Mix it up

To ensure your look is fabulous, mix your cheaper clothes with designer pieces, high-quality accessories and vintage finds.

Remember, cheap clothes are not disposable

Buying cheap is no reason for purchasing clothes you won't wear. Fabrics have been manufactured at a cost to the environment and people have worked to make the clothes. So ask yourself if the garment you like really suits you and if you will really wear it. If the answers are no, do not buy it, even if it is the same price as a latte.

Secret Address Book

While Parisians like to be understated, they also enjoy standing out from the crowd. Not so much by wearing loud clothes, but rather by being noticed for their unique taste in everything. Nothing pleases us more than being asked, in a tone of admiration, "Where did you get this?" A tiny ring will be appreciated as much as a gorgeous dress.

Let me share with you the clever Parisian tricks for shopping differently from your neighbour when the internet is worldwide and the streets of every city in the world contain the same stores. I have also included a few favourites from my very own address book, so should you ever find yourself wandering the streets of Paris…

1. Find out the secret on- and offline retailers

Discovering secret boutiques and new designers always requires a bit of research on your part. I recommend you:

• Read the magazines that often feature young brands.

• Click on the recommendations of your favourite influencers (sometimes they help emerging designers get publicity).

• Listen carefully to your fashionable friends when they talk about what's cool and new.

• Be bold and ask those same friends where they got their clothes (if there is no privacy policy, that should do it).

• Ask someone living in the city what their secret addresses in town are.

• Take different routes around your city and you may discover some great ateliers and boutiques (works for Paris).

2. Shop local while abroad

Who would have thought the "tourist T-shirt" would one day become a style statement? When on your travels, look out for items you wouldn't get at home. It could be gorgeous fabrics from India, a silk top from China, a bracelet from a local jeweller, jewellery replicas in a museum store, a sports brand jacket, a pretty bathing suit at the market or even a child's watch.

3. Look for unique vintage pieces

Search on eBay or other online platforms. Try to be precise in your requests, by mentioning velvet boots or a snakeskin belt, for example. You could get unique pieces for affordable prices. Another method is to search for a famous brand before browsing the results.

In the city, head for vintage and second-hand stores, which often have more designer pieces than you would find in thrift stores.

My go-to boutiques

For beautiful gloves
- Maison Fabre
Jardins du Palais Royal,
128-129, Galerie de Valois, 75001 Paris
www.maisonfabre.com

My favourite hat store
- Mademoiselle Chapeaux
15 Rue des Tournelles, 75004 Paris
www.mademoisellechapeaux.com

For fantastic jewellery
- Hod
104 Rue Vieille du Temple, 75003 Paris
www.hod-boutique.com

- Matières à Réflexions
19 Rue de Poitou, Paris
www.matieresareflexion.com

My go-to hairstylist
- Les Dada East
52 Rue Trousseau, 75011 Paris
www.instagram.com/lesdadaeast

Amazing underwear selection
- Bon Marché
24 Rue de Sèvres, 75007 Paris
www.24sevres.com

For thrift treasures
- Kiliwatch rue Tiquetonne
64 Rue Tiquetonne, 75002 Paris
kiliwatch.paris/vintage

- Louise Paris
5 Rue du Chateau d'eau, 75010 Paris
www.louiseparis.fr

March over here for shoes galore
- Boutique 58M
Rue Montmartre, 75002 Paris
www.58m.fr

Index

Picture Credits

The publishers would like to acknowledge and thank the following for kindly supplying images for use in this book.

Adeline Rapon @adelinerapon 212, 220; photo Gael Rapon 9

Candice Lake candicelake.com/@candicelake 34

Eve Dupouy www.beaauuu.com 169

photo **Fanny Dussol** for MissPandora.fr/@louiseebelpandora 231

Gisele Isnerdy Giseleisnerdy.fr/@giseleisnerdy 48, 66, 89, 93, 106; photo Amy Ta 47; photo Swann and the Berries @swannandtheberries 37; photo Albane de Marnhac 87

photo **Guillaume Gaudet** for MissPandora.fr/@louiseebelpandora 81

Irma Notorahardjo Refashiongallery.com/@refashiongallery/rollingpearl.com 132, 141, 156

Photo **Jude Foulard** for MissPandora.fr/@louiseebelpandora 30

@juliettekitsch 27, 51, 57, 59; @plusmaevane 120

@leontine_29 78, 126, 139

Madame Virgule madamevirgule.com/@madamevirgule 38, 123, 161, 227

Marie @intoyourcloset photo Clara Ferrand 101

Onayza Sayah @onayza, photo Julien Dabadie @julien_dabadie 222

Paulien Riemis polienne.com/@paulienriemis 113, 117, 124, 129

Paz Halabi Rodriguez pazhalabirodriguez.com/@pazhalabirodriguez 24, 69

Violaine Olga Madeleine @viou 12, 19, 159, 219, 224

Additional credits

Getty Images Bertrand Rindoff Petroff 118; Bertrand Rindoff Petroff/Pierre Suu 155; Christian Vierig 75, 152; Darren Gerrish/WireImage 33; Dominique Charriau/WireImage 178; Edward Berthelot 131, 145, 176, 233; Foc Khan/WireImage 180; Francois G Durand/WireImage 62; Francos Durand/Getty Images for Paramount Pictures 114; Ian Gavan/WireImage 165; Jacopo Raule/GC Images 217; Jamie McCarthy/Getty Images for Marc Jacobs 187; Josiah Kamau/BuzzFoto 11; Kirstin Sinclair 64; Marc Piasecki/GC Images 41; Marc Piasecki/WireImage 98, 179; Melodie Jeng 90, 110, 186; Pierre Suu/GC Images 85, 181, 185; Stephane Cardinale/Corbis 76; Sylvain Lefevre 215; Taxi 204; Timur Emek 23; Venturelli/WireImage 177; **REX Shutterstock** Olivier Degoulange 29; Silvia Olsen 52; Wayne Tippetts 105, 146; **Shutterstock** DKSStyle 61, 102, 170; Huang Zheng 20

Thomas Michard www.thomphotos.paris 7, 54, 82, 142, 162, 182, 184

Illustrations: **Judith van den Hoek**

Acknowledgments

To my mum for instilling in me a love of clothing. To Angèle who encouraged me to become a personal stylist. To my sisters Esther, Cassandre, Olga, Naomi and Zoé and my dad whom I spent the summer with while I was writing this book. To Agathe, Léa and Quentin who supported me while I was writing. To my clients for teaching me more about women every day. Thank you Joy, Malvika, Pamela, Anne-Lise, Marion, Martine, Hélène, Isabelle, Catherine, Louise, Julie, Vanessa, Helen and all the beautiful people I met over the years…To my blog readers for following my fashion advice and sharing their comments with me. To my hairdresser grandmother for teaching me a thing or two about hair styling and to her nephew – and now master hairstylist – Vinz. To Anne-Sophie, a former trend forecasting agency colleague who is now a marketing expert in lingerie and underwear. To Sarina, who studied at IFM with me and is now successfully running her own luxury beauty box and cosmetic brand. To Ingrid, Cécile, Emmanuelle, Anaïs and Farrah for welcoming me into their closets and discussing their relationship with fashion. To Thomas, who photographed them and me. To the teachers at Institut Français de la Mode for passing on their knowledge. To Sabine and Thierry for hosting me during a writing retreat. To Martine and Pascal for their support.

Merci